T5-DHC-048

The Miracle Road

Jerry & Annie Shaw

WINEPRESS WP PUBLISHING

© 1998 by Jerry and Annie Shaw. All rights reserved

Printed in the United States of America

Packaged by WinePress Publishing, PO Box 1406, Mukilteo, WA 98275. The views expressed or implied in this work do not necessarily reflect those of WinePress Publishing. Ultimate design, content, and editorial accuracy of this work is the responsibility of the author(s).

No part of this publication may be reproduced, stored in a retrieval system or transmitted in any way by any means, electronic, mechanical, photocopy, recording or otherwise, without the prior permission of the copyright holder except as provided by USA copyright law.

All scripture is from the King James Version of the Bible.

ISBN 1-57921-119-4
Library of Congress Catalog Card Number: 98-60707

Contents

About This Book

———≈≈≈≈≈———

We dedicate this book of many blessings to three saintly sisters.

First, to Ethel Gorman to whom the Holy Spirit gave a word of knowledge several years ago. She informed us that we would write this book. Years later we supernaturally sensed that *now* is the time to write *The Miracle Road*, and upon phoning home, found that Sister Ethel had gone home to be with Jesus.

Second, to Mildred Westhover whose story is so unique we felt led to include it in a chapter in this book. You'll enjoy reading "A Saint."

Third, to Martha Crowley, Sister Annie's mother, whom we both loved. She recently left to be with her first love, Jesus.

We pray you will enjoy riding with us through the cities, towns, and villages from the Atlantic to the Pacific Oceans; from the Arctic to Old Mexico; through almost every state and province of the USA and Canada.

So climb in the cab with the Holy Spirit and us. It's a good day to travel *The Miracle Road*.

Jerry and Annie

Along this earth, walk many people who pass through our lives. Some leave their footprints engraved forever on our hearts. Our friend Peter Pulis is just such a person. Thanks Peter, for praying and believing truely, the steps of a good man are ordered of the Lord. (Ps. 37:23)

The Calls

⚡〰〰⚡

The powerful jet engines roared like caged lions as the 747 shook violently in expectation for takeoff. A rush of emotions soared through me. I was seated over the left wing and my wife, Annie, was assigned the seat in front of me. Over the intercom a voice said, "Fasten your seat belt, and stand by for takeoff." The jet went from zero to takeoff speed in just seconds. No matter how many times I've flown, I always feel the need to pray "dear Lord, help us get off this runway safely."

We did, and the plane climbed to new heights! I looked out the window through a hole in the clouds for one last look at the city of St. John's, Newfoundland. The noise of the plane consumed me. My concentration was broken by a voice that said, "This is your flight captain. We are flying at 13,000 feet. The air temperature is twenty-one degrees below zero outside your air-conditioned cabin; our air speed is 440 miles per hour. Our estimated time of arrival at Halifax International Airport is one hour and thirty-five minutes. Have a good day, and thank you for flying Air Canada."

The man beside me seemed to be asleep. Who could blame him? There wasn't much to do, so I followed his lead and drifted off to sleep. All of a sudden, I heard a voice say, "I'm sending you back to this island to minister for me." I glanced at the man beside me, but he hadn't moved; his eyes were still closed. So it surely wasn't him who spoke. Then the voice came again with volume and authority.

"I'm sending you back to the island to minister." (See John 10:27.) The intercom again broke into my thoughts when a voice said, "Please fasten your seat belts. We will be landing at the Halifax International Airport very shortly. Please remain seated until the airplane comes to a complete stop."

The wheels touched the runway and the plane slowed to a feel-safe speed. I again said, "Thank you, Lord." We picked up our luggage and made our way to the car.

As the lights of the airport were fading in the rear view mirror, I said, "Annie, God has spoken to me. He said, 'I'm sending you back to the island to minister.'" You could cut the silence with a knife. Then after a while, she turned to me and said (Annie recalls her words at that moment), "maybe you, but not me."

I'm only a woman. I didn't want God to move us out of where we were, but Jerry kept saying, "Annie, God is calling us into the ministry."

It took a while to sink in. I kind of ignored Jerry. I just didn't know what had happened to him. And though he didn't push the issue, he didn't quite let it sleep. Every now and then he would say, "Annie, God is calling us into the ministry."

I said, "Well, Jerry, I know how you feel; I'll be here. You go ahead, I'll be here. I'll be waiting here, you know. I'll keep the home fires burning. I'll be a light in the window. Whatever, but don't ask me to leave home." Just let me bloom where God has planted me! But at night when I went to bed, I couldn't sleep. I would hear Jerry's words echoing, "Annie, God has called us into the ministry." I had no peace. It got to me really bad. I wished Jerry had never said that to me. I could not stop thinking about it. So I called my friends and said, "Would you please pray for us? Jerry thinks that we are being called into the ministry, but I just know that we're not. Would you please pray that God will open his eyes?" They said, "Yes, we will pray."

About that time, we got a new pastor. He was an English fellow who had grown up in South Africa. I now placed my burden on him, a man who was trying to adjust to our way of life. I phoned him and said, "Pastor, Jerry and I need to see you right away." Wouldn't you know? When the pastor arrived, Jerry had gone to get supplies. So I talked to him, pulling no punches. I told him all the reasons why I was positive that we were not called into the ministry. I summed it up and said, "Pastor, my husband thinks that we are called into the ministry, but I know we're not.

"Brother, I'm involved in the church. You need me, Pastor. Who is going to teach my Sunday school class? You know it, Brother, you need me. Willing workers in the church are few and far between. You know that."

He responded, "Well, Sister, maybe you're not called seeing as you feel that way." And he left it like that. So when Jerry came home, I said, "Jerry, the Pastor has said 'maybe we're not called.'" It felt good to have the pastor on my side. It kind of felt like almost having God on my side. But I still had no peace. And I tell you, if God is calling you, amen, he loves you. He knows what is best for you. Where, then, was my peace that God promises his children? (See John 14:27.)

So we would pray, "Please, Lord, speak to us. Open the eyes of our understanding." Night after night we knelt and prayed. We started praying together right after we gave our hearts to Jesus. I got saved first, then Jerry, and we started to believe God together. So we'd pray together.

God is so patient with his children. We would pray for our brothers and sisters. We found in the Bible where it said, "Pray ye therefore the Lord of the harvest . . ." (Matt. 9:38). It said, ". . . look on the fields; for they are white already to harvest" (John 4:35), and we believed it. The Word reads, ". . . the laborers are few" (Matt. 9:37). Amen? So Jerry and I would pray our regular prayers and one of us would say, "Oh yes, send forth laborers."

BE IN READINESS

You have got to be ready to do what you're praying for. If you pray to God, you had better be ready for him to answer in his way. So I knew I had to be in readiness.

FEET TO MY PRAYER

One morning I got up knowing full well that God had not called us into the ministry. But still I did not have any peace, which was strange, because the first thing the Lord did for me when I got saved was to give me his wonderful peace. So much, in fact, that I didn't need tranquilizers, sedatives, or sleeping pills any longer. I was totally delivered of man-made crutches. But now, my peace was gone! Sure, I didn't need tranquilizers; my nerves weren't bad or anything. I was just uneasy. Then one morning, I got up and was about to begin the day, but before I started, I prayed, "Lord, if you are really calling us into the ministry, I need to hear from you. I need to hear from heaven, not from Jerry, not from my friends, not from the pastor. I need to hear from you, Lord!" It is true, God still speaks to the listening heart.

I was cleaning up around our restaurant when the Holy Spirit dropped this nugget into my heart: "make full proof of thy ministry." Hallelujah! Hallelujah! Three times my Lord spoke to me. Three times, because I didn't know if I was just remembering something I heard in a message or not. ". . . make full proof of thy ministry" (2 Tim. 4:5). David said, "Thy word have I hid in mine heart . . . " (Ps. 119:11).

God says obedience is better than sacrifice. Our earthly mother and father taught us that we must be obedient. And it follows that above anything else, God wants us to be obedient. Anyway, I thought it sounded like something from the Bible. It seemed to me that it should be in the Bible. So I got my concordance and looked it up. I found where it was written, "watch thou." And all of a sudden Jesus spoke to me through his Word. I read, "But watch thou in all things, endure afflictions . . . " (2 Tim. 4:5).

I didn't know what that meant then, but I do now. I know after so much trouble with our truck, illnesses, and such things that we must be willing to serve God through such afflictions. (See 2 Tim. 4:2.) ". . . do the work of an evangelist. Make full proof of thy ministry" (2 Tim. 2:5). I felt a shiver of truth, something clicked; something happened inside, something changed and I ran to find Jerry. I said, "Guess what, Jerry? God has called us into the ministry."

"Really," my husband said. "No kidding," he chuckled.

"B-b-but you don't understand. It wasn't you after all, it was *God*, God, God, God . . . "

Of course, everything was anything but cut and dried. True, God had confirmed his call, but he never said when to go. So we waited, not wanting to get ahead of God. Where he leads us, we will follow.

In his time, he again spoke to our spirits—a holy nudge, not unlike the prophet Isaiah received—saying, ". . . Go . . ." (See Isa. 6:9).

However a message was delivered via the Holy Spirit that informed those who needed to know we were . . .

Coming Soon

The Word says, ". . . Go ye into all the world . . . " (Mark 16:15). ". . . do the work of an evangelist . . ." (2 Tim. 4:5). "Be my hand extended." There's scripture after scripture instructing us who have been called on what to do. For those who heed the leading of God's Holy Spirit, the rewards are manifold. He said he would "supply all your need" (Phil. 4:19). God's word is positive. He will provide for those he calls.

HIT THE ROAD FOR JESUS

We knew in our spirits that God had called us. So with our little four-cylinder car and a one-wheel trailer yoked to the rear bumper, we hit the road for Jesus.

The ropes that held the giant ferry boat captive, were loosed. The scream of the whistle signaled our departure, sounding through the fog that enveloped the wharf. With a roar that caused the salt water to churn, she moved off into the night, her bow sharply cutting its mark in the icy North Atlantic waters.

"I'm sending you back to the island to minister," was for me, no longer just a still, small voice that echoed in my mind. At last, we were en route to the battlefield. Now we were doing as the Lord had requested. We had stepped out in faith. (See Heb. 11:1-39.)

All night long, the boat broke its way through the heavy ice in the Gulf of Saint Lawrence, sometimes getting bogged down, then backing up. Then with the ice breaking bow, it rammed its way to open water victory.

Morning light didn't yet grant us a warm welcome as we drove off the gulf ferry at Port-Aux-Basques. The town itself hadn't yet awakened enough to be friendly, but the sign on the landlocked schooner, placed there by the province of Newfoundland, said it all in three words: Welcome to Newfoundland.

The barrenness of the rugged coastline gave way to strong stands of spruce forest as we motored east across the island. The roads were rough, and I really mean rough! Frost heaves and potholes. We'd try to miss a bad spot here, only to hit another that we failed to see. Sometimes we'd see signs reading: rough sections ahead. Yes indeed, they really meant it; they were rough! We probably should have stopped for the night at a motel or hotel because we were bone tired. We didn't get much sleep on the boat, and we had been driving all day. Overly tired was much more how we felt. There wasn't much traffic that night. The towns were few and many miles between. Annie had fallen asleep with her head turned toward the window. I wished I could grab a few minutes shut-eye. I cracked the window to allow the fresh air to keep me ticking just a little bit longer. But even the cold air wasn't quite enough to do it. We were rounding a long curve in the highway when I fell fast asleep at the wheel. It was then that I heard a voice call me. "Jerry!" I snapped back to life just in time. Our car and trailer had left the pavement and were headed for the woods! I yanked us back onto the highway. Thank the Lord for traveling mercy!

I have mentioned before that our call to the ministry came at thirteen thousand feet above the rugged rock called Newfoundland when his voice said, "I'm sending you back to this island to minister for me." Our calls to the ministry were now reality. We were tired, but happy in the Lord. Hours later, we pulled into the small, south-coast fishing town of Grand Bank. At best, just a small dot on the map. We met the local pastor, who welcomed us with open arms and told us that we were expected. Annie and I looked at each other.

Did he say, expected? Expected? How would anyone know we were coming? We never told anyone. Expected?

Then he continued. It seems that in a word of prophecy at a church rally three weeks before, someone had spoken in tongues and another had interpreted it. The Holy Spirit had announced that two people, matching our descriptions, were coming soon!

God knows and will direct your path.

While we were in Tennessee, God had added to the two of us. A desire of our hearts—twelve ounces of pure joy! A Chihuahua named . . .

Tripsy

TRIPSY'S BAPTISM

We loaded much, much more than we'd ever need into our little car and pulled out of the driveway, headed south on our first real vacation since we were married. Before we left the yard, we prayed asking the Lord to go before us. We asked him to lead us to born-again Christian businesses on this trip. For years we operated our restaurant and live lobster pound, so we knew first-hand how difficult it is to operate a Christian business, and we wanted to support them. As always, God directed our path. We ate in Christian restaurants, slept in Christian motels, we even gassed up in service stations that sold Bibles over the counter. Truly God has sheep in many pastures. (See Ps. 79:13). All we have to do is ask God to lead us.

OUR HEART'S DESIRE

We'd always wanted a small dog. We knew that it was only a matter of time. If we kept our eyes open, we'd eventually see a sign reading: Chihuahuas for Sale. Sure enough, one day we were driving through a little southern town when we spotted a hand-drawn sign that read: Chihuahuas for Sale. So we stopped to check it out. We found a lady, fully dressed in winter clothes, an old scarf wrapped tightly around her face. Her eyes and nose were all that were visible. She looked cold! We asked her about her dogs, and she showed us the one Chihuahua she had left. The runt of the litter she told us.

"It's cute," we said. "How much are you asking?" She told us the price, but it was more than we wanted to spend. We never want to miss an opportunity to tell someone about Jesus, so we shared with the lady telling why we had come to her little town.

"We're on vacation—a second honeymoon," we told her. "We're born-again Christians. We love Jesus." We added that Jesus loves her as well. We said we'd be happy to pray for her.

"I've been sick," she told us. "Yes, I need prayer."

Here was an open door. She welcomed prayer. So we prayed for her health, her family, and her business. God must have spoken to her during the prayer because she decided to let us have that little dog at a price that even surprised her. As we paid her, she said with disbelief in her voice, "Why, I've never sold a dog so cheaply before!" Of course we thanked her with all our hearts, and we thanked Jesus as well. Then we put the little dog in the car and drove on toward Nashville. It didn't take us long to fall in love with the little dog. We named her Tripsy. She weighed in at twelve ounces.

That night at the motel in Nashville we washed her in the sink, laughing again at the comment one man had made about her, "Why, she's no bigger than a bar of soap!" She wasn't big, that's for sure. She quickly adjusted to her new life with us, and we to her. We'd sometimes stop along the highway to get ourselves a take-out coffee with an extra coffee creamer for Tripsy, who was so small she could stick her face and most of her head into the creamer and slurp it dry!

Storm Bound

Overnight, an ice storm hit Nashville, Tennessee. What a disaster! It tied up everything. Only the brave and foolish dared to venture out on the roads—we were two of them. But we had the roads to ourselves to explore music city.

We noticed a sign flashing off and on: New Testament tapes—$19.95. Annie stayed in the car while I went in to check it out. It turned out to be a Christian recording studio. Only the owner was there, a short, heavy-set man with a pleasant voice and a warm friendly Tennessee smile. Since this was Nashville and I had written a few gospel songs, I thought, "Hey, I'll speak to him about it." So I did. "I have them on a cassette tape in the car. Would you listen?"

"Sure," he said, "Bring them in." He listened, and I waited for his comment. Finally he said, "Those are good songs. You should record them." I said, "I'd like to, but I don't have a lot of money. I don't even have my guitar to get these songs ready." He said, "Here, I'll loan you mine." It was a beautiful handmade Gramer guitar—almost priceless.

We booked another night at the motel, went to work on the music, and somehow got ready the songs that we thought we should record. But the next morning I woke up full of doubt as to whether we should proceed on this. "You see," Satan whispered in my ear, "That's a lot of money. 'A fool and his money are soon parted.' Who would want to buy your tapes?" I managed to keep it to myself, but truthfully, I was troubled. Although the studio owner had worked out a way that we could pay him later, I still felt this was a lot of money, more than we could afford.

As I carried his guitar into the studio, I made what I thought to be my final decision. I broke it to him this way: "Brother Beavers, because of our lack of money, we better put this off for perhaps another year. I appreciate your kind offer. Thank you very much." I turned on my heel and walked toward the door when suddenly I heard a voice say, **"If you don't do it now, you never will."** Of course, I realized it was his voice, but never had I heard such authority. I took it to be directly from God. I turned and said, "How long would it take you to get the musicians?"

"Well because of the ice storm, everyone's stuck in town. Probably about one o'clock."

I said, "OK. Let's do it. We'll come back then."

When we returned, the studio was alive with the sounds of instruments being tuned to perfection. The best of Nashville's musicians were about to help us record this tape for Jesus.

A ministry was being born, and of course, Tripsy was part of the team. She traveled with us from town to town, city to city. Wherever we went, we'd sing the songs of Zion, preach the word, and pray for the sick. When the services were over, we'd come back to our trailer and there she'd be, always wagging her own special welcome.

Tripsy Missing

It was a beautiful, warm sunny day in St. Anthony, New-foundland. Annie and a new sister in the Lord who had given her heart to Jesus the night before, were sitting on the back steps of a church when our little dog Tripsy turned up missing. Annie called for her over and over, but she didn't come. They looked everywhere but couldn't find her. With panic in her voice, Annie came crying to me, "Jerry, Tripsy's gone! We have looked everywhere that we could think of. We searched and searched, but it was no good. We couldn't find her." I joined the search party and re-searched but came up empty. No Tripsy.

It was about two hours later while I was on the phone inside the church calling a local radio station asking them to announce a lost dog, our Tripsy, when I thought I heard a small, faint bark. At first I thought I was hearing things. Wishful thinking! But something inside me said, "Search again." So I began to search inch by inch, continually call-ing out her name. "Here, Tripsy!" But there was nothing, not one single sound. "Here Tripsy!" I searched my way from the back of the church to the front and up into the pulpit area. There I found they had a sunken baptismal tank with steps leading down into it. I didn't want to leave one single stone unturned, so I walked down the steps onto the floor of the tank. All of a sudden, a small, frightened Chi-huahua named Tripsy, came out from behind the steps to royally welcome me! Amen!

Sometimes our well-intended seed falls on stony areas where the rocks of life prevent it from taking root. We often pray that we will have another opportunity, and in God's time we no doubt will. Perhaps today, perhaps tomorrow, or . . .

Maybe Later

He never said it would be easy, just worth it. Many are the demands on a road evangelist. God intends for us to be like Paul, all things to all people. A men's group, which was about to go on visitation, came to the trailer requesting that I come with them to meet a man who had been in a car accident.

"He's lost both of his legs above the knees. He needs prayer. He sits most of the time in a wheelchair," they explained. "Will you come?

"His daughter is a member of the church, and her heart's desire is to see her father saved. So she asked us, the men of the church, to help. We tried repeatedly to lead him to Jesus, but so far he has not made a commitment. So we thought, 'Let's ask the evangelist to come with us. Maybe he can help.'" They wanted me to bring a guitar, sing a song, and just share. I said, "Yes, I'll be glad to."

I went to his house with the men's group. We were invited in. He looked forward to these Tuesday meetings when he would have someone to talk to. He enjoyed the company. His mind was good; he sang with us "Amazing Grace, how sweet the sound, that saved a wretch like me." I talked to him over the evening about Jesus, asking him several times point blank, "Have you given your heart to Jesus?" "No," he said, "No, I haven't." I would say, "Well, you need to. Can we pray together? Just a short prayer. You can give your life to Jesus right now." He would say, "Not now, maybe later."

I felt in my spirit that this man did not have a lot of time, so during the evening I tried repeatedly to bring him to the point where I could lead him to Jesus because I sensed an urgency; it had to be done quickly. Each time that we would get close to the subject, he would say, "Not now, maybe later." Many times people ask the question, "what is the unforgivable sin?" The unforgivable sin is the rejection of Jesus Christ. By not accepting, we're rejecting.

We left town and continued on the road for Jesus. On we went, church after church, town after town. It was almost a year before we were back that way again. I asked about him at the men's group. They said, "Funny you should ask about him. His mind is completely gone. You can't talk to him anymore. He can't carry a conversation. He isn't able to read or talk, he's just a vegetable." I recalled him saying to me, "maybe later, maybe later, maybe later, maybe later."

FOOTNOTE

". . . now is the accepted time . . . of salvation." (2 Cor. 6:2). Anyone who puts off accepting Jesus into their life allows their heart to harden. The Word says, ". . . My spirit shall not always strive with man . . ." (Genesis 6:3). Even taking our next breath depends upon him, amen. *Now* is the accepted time of salvation.

Our gifts to God are like money held in trust by an insurance company. God holds them on deposit until dividend day when our need is met. (See Phil. 4:19.)

One sure thing—God is . . .

No Man's Debtor

‗‗‗∾∿∾∿‗‗‗

When you pull a forty-foot trailer along the highway, you expect things to go wrong. After all, it's man-made, and everything man-made is eventually recycled or trashed. As we were pulling into Cornerbrook, Newfoundland, that's when the brakes went out on our trailer. Thank God we were close to the bottom of the hill. There was only one trailer repair shop in the area and they told us they'd be happy to fix our brakes if we had a week to ten days. They were swamped.

"Check the wires," they suggested. "It could be just a short. The blue wire is the brake. Good luck."

I'm not a mechanic, but I followed their advice. I couldn't find anything wrong, so I did the only thing I know to do when everything else fails—I prayed. I cried out to God. "Help!" Then it came to me. We were at the foot of the hill anyway. It's uphill to the plateau. We certainly didn't need any brakes to climb a hill. I knew that the twenty-five miles between Cornerbrook and Deer Lake was all flat country. The truck brakes should be able to handle it. After prayer, we climbed the hill and rolled along the flat land to the town of Deer Lake. We had pre-arranged a meeting with the pastor of a full gospel church. We pulled into the parking area, and I spoke to the secretary.

"I'd like to talk to your pastor, use your photocopier, and, do you have a mechanic that attends your church?" She said, "Go ahead, use the photocopier. The pastor won't be back until late this afternoon, and, yes, there's a mechanic who's part of our church. In fact, I just finished speaking with him on the phone," she smiled. "Believe it or not, he's on his way here right now." Just as she finished talking, he arrived.

"This is Johnny," she said. She briefed him a little about our problem as she introduced us. "Johnny can fix anything," she added.

THE HAND OF GOD

"Sure, I can help you," he said. "Follow me." He took us to a little out-of-the-way place where some men were working on heavy vehicles. We parked the trailer, and he went to work on our brakes. He found so many things wrong that he said, "The Lord has certainly been looking after you. Look at this." He showed us parts on the undercarriage of the trailer that were worn thin.

"No problem," he said. "I'll make new parts." And he did.

"It looks like the hand of God was truly upon you," he said. He worked all afternoon until close to six o'clock, and still wasn't finished. So he said, "Come with me."

He took us by car to his house. His wife was a small, bubbly Newfoundlander who made us very welcome. She opened up her heart and then she opened her refrigerator to feed us. After supper, she decided to come back with Johnny while he continued working. Finally, at about ten o'clock that night, he pronounced it done. I thought, "How in the world am I ever going to pay for this?" We needed a Philippians 4:19. Help, Lord!

I said, "It's always a pleasure to pay for things like this; I hope you take Visa?"

"Oh," he said, "there's no charge whatsoever for this. You're a servant of God! Are you having meetings in the area?"

"Yes, we are," I told him and gave him the time and place for our meeting the following night. He said, "I believe I can go."

The following night we were at a church about twenty miles from there when Johnny, our mechanic friend, walked in with his family. They sat in a seat near the front. The church was jam-packed with people who had come expecting to receive from God.

Many times Jesus said, "Thy faith hath made thee whole." (Luke 8:48). Faith in God can move a mighty mountain. Faith in God can calm the troubled sea. Faith will make the desert like a fountain. Faith will bring the victory!

People were coming to the front for prayer. The Holy Spirit was touching them. One by one, as they fell to the floor slain in the spirit, they were being healed of all sorts of sickness and affliction. Some people were healed as they sat in their seat, some were healed while walking to the front of the church. God was moving!

At the end of the service, Johnny said to me, "You're going east on the island?"

"Yes, we are."

"Be sure to contact me on the way back. You have to go through this town anyway, there's no way around it. No matter what time it is, night or day, call me or stop in. I have to talk to you."

About two months later, we were finally leaving the island of Newfoundland. Winter was closing in on us. Snow had arrived and our trailer walls were too thin to keep out the cold, so we knew it was time to head south. We had just received a letter from a pastor in Florida who invited us to come to his area. It must be the Lord, we thought. On our way back, before leaving the island, as promised, we stopped to see Johnny.

"It's been more than two months since you were here," he said. "That night when arthritis was called out, I was totally healed, but I had to be sure before I told anyone."

FOOTNOTE

Johnny the Mechanic would not accept a thin dime for all the work he did on our trailer, but God had a payment that was far beyond anything money could buy. Johnny planted his labor as seed for his need. Johnny's arthritis was totally healed! God is no man's debtor.

We serve a faithful God who every now and again wants us to step out of our comfortable boat and walk on life's ocean. Like Peter, we, too, will become confident in Jesus, as hand in hand, step by step, he leads us . . .

From Doubter to Shouter

‒‒‒‒〰〰〰‒‒‒‒

It's always a privilege to minister at a camp meeting. People seem to relax and open themselves up to allow the Spirit to minister to them. Gone are the starchy old shirts and stiff ties. In their place is a willingness to receive. We were having beautiful meetings with a service in the morning and another in the evening.

Many people were receiving from God; it was a powerful, wonderful, glorious move of God that seemed to intensify daily. One day it came to my attention that there was a man who was sick unto death only a short distance away. He was staying in the house of his friend. There's no denying the Holy Spirit. The still, small voice of God spoke to my heart and said, "You are to go and pray for him." I said to Annie, "God has spoken. We must see this man and pray for him."

We went to the house where he was staying, knocked on the door, and, upon entering, met his wife. We told her that we had come to pray for her husband. She said, "Fine, I'll go see if he's awake." We were invited into the room where he was lying in bed. We talked to him, telling him we had come to pray. He welcomed prayer. As I laid hands on him, I had a word of knowledge from the Lord.

"Brother, the reason you have not been healed is because you are full of doubt." At that point, his wife spoke up, voicing her opinions. "That's anything but true. He is not full of doubt," she said. "Stanley's a born-again Christian. There's no earthly reason in the world why you should say that." Her every word was aimed straight at me! "If there's one thing I know for sure, it's that he's not full of doubt!" she pounded her point home. When she stopped talking, he spoke up again, "Yes, it's true. I've had an awful lot of doubt."

We began to pray for him. I laid my hand on his toe and I prayed, "Lord, in the name of Jesus, please help him surrender this doubt so we can pray for the specific problem in his body." As we prayed, we could feel that something was happening. Suddenly, everyone in the entire room felt lighter, including myself. Something had lifted, something had left— it had to be the spirit of doubt. We then began to pray for the needs in his body and for God to touch him. God moved miraculously in that room. We had gone the extra mile, gone a few steps farther for Jesus, and, Jesus, never to be outdone, had come via the Holy Spirit right into this bedroom.

It's a Miracle

Within the hour, not only had he gotten out of bed, he was splitting wood in the back yard! There's no way to deny a true miracle from God. There's no way to keep someone who knows beyond any shadow of doubt that he's healed, quiet. He's excited and wants the whole world to know.

Later, he came to the trailer asking if there was anything he could do. He was soon able to go back to work. The town that had employed him willingly took him back after receiving the doctor's report that declared him totally healed.

About a year went by. We were back in the same area for another meeting. Our "shouter" was able to come. As soon as I saw him, I knew that he was still healed. Praise God! He was willing to give his testimony.

This is what he said: "I was three-quarters dead, like Hezekiah in Second Kings—sick unto death. I had been sawing wood when my left arm went dead. I stopped work, and by the next day it seemed better, so I tried some gardening. Right away, the arm quit again. It went stone dead. My wife is the worrying type, so I didn't feel that I should tell her. Sure enough, a few days later, I felt much better, so I tried cutting wood again. The same thing happened: dead again. I went to the doctor, and he checked me over. Shaking his head, he said, "It's beyond me." He sent me to specialists to investigate my strange condition. They agreed that I should stop work. For how long they didn't know, possibly months! 'But don't worry, we'll get to the bottom of it,' they said.

When Man Quits, God Starts

"They tried everything known to man and medicine. Finally, they admitted they didn't know what was wrong. Well, it came camp meeting time, and I went just to please my wife. I'm thankful that I did! On the second day of camp, Brother Shaw heard that I was very sick. He and Sister Annie came to the house. I was too weak to get up. Brother Shaw said that God had sent them to lay hands on me, and to pray. He said that I was full of doubt about God and healing but that he would pray and I would be healed. He laid hands on me and prayed. I felt God's healing power surge through me. He took me by the right hand and pulled me from the bed. Praise the Lord, like the man in Acts 3:10, I've been leaping, walking, and praising the Lord ever since! Oh, I've had more tests, like EEG's, X-rays, CAT scans; in fact, every test they could put me through. They all proved negative. I'm no longer three-quarters dead. I'm one-hundred percent alive! I'm no longer a doubter, praise God, I'm a 'shouter'! Hallelujah Amen!"

God never said it would be easy—just worth it!

Jesus spoke from that old rugged cross, "Father forgive them. They know not what they do."

We must follow in his footsteps, always willing to turn the other cheek and be ready to extend a heart full of love and . . .

Forgiveness

～～～～～

We'd only been saved about a year. We were growing in our faith—God had done so much for us. The Word of God says he began a good work in us and he would complete it. He had to clean many of the rough edges, and he had his way of doing it, praise God! His way worked.

We owned a seafood restaurant in which we worked, Jerry and I, with our two teenage children. We really didn't need extra help most of the time. We were members of our home church and we were busy people!

There was a lady that attended our church who was always in need. We didn't know her history or background, but it seemed she didn't have victory most of the time. She always had a financial need. To see a brother or sister in need and to not attempt to help them is not our idea of a Christian, so we decided to offer her a job in our restaurant. She seemed grateful and came to work with us.

Carole was a very troubled lady. She wasn't working with us long when we found that she was never satisfied. Carole always brought many problems to work. We tried to help her as much as we could. We prayed for her and did whatever we felt God would have us do, but still she wasn't happy. Finally, she decided that she wouldn't work with us any longer. When she left, she didn't go nicely. She was a hurting lady and had a vengeful spirit. She decided that she would vent some anger on us.

We didn't owe her anything when she left; in fact, she owed us. About a week later, she came back into our restaurant. Her face reflected her mood. First she told Jerry off, then told me off as well. James 3:5-8 mentions the tongue. ". . . the tongue is a little member . . . and it is set on fire of hell . . . the tongue can no man tame . . . it is . . . full of deadly poison." There are so many things people can say when they are angry and hurt. I finally reached my breaking point where I just couldn't take any more. As a Christian, this was the first time I'd had to face something like this.

I told Carole, "You have no right to come against us like this." Hot words were exchanged, but it did no good. Fire cannot quench fire. After she left, I called my pastor's wife and I told her what had happened. To my surprise she said, "Annie, we know about this sister. We know that she's very troubled. Just forgive her."

Then the Spirit of God began to speak to my heart and said, "I want you to ask her forgiveness." I thought I was hearing things. I thought, "I don't need to ask her forgiveness. I've only tried to help this woman. There's no way I need to ask her forgiveness." But I had no peace in my heart. That's how it is when the still, small voice of God is dealing with your spirit, prompting you over and over again. "I want you to ask her forgiveness." Finally, to get peace, I said, "OK. I'll ask her forgiveness." But I didn't want to see her face to face, so I called her on the telephone. I said,

"Sister, I want to ask your forgiveness." She said to me, "Sure, Annie, I'll forgive you."

Well, I nearly blew it right there, because in my heart I believed that it was she who should be asking my forgiveness. But the next words she spoke made me realize how much God loves all of us in spite of our faults and failings. The next words she said were, "I want you to forgive me, too." I said, "Yes, of course I'll forgive you."

The instant I said, "I forgive you," I felt like the Lord had poured a bottle of oil over my head. I know now what David meant when he said, "Behold, how good and pleasant it is for brethren to dwell together in unity! It is like the precious ointment upon the head, that ran down upon the beard, even Aaron's beard: that went down to the skirts of his garments" (Psalm 133:1-2). It was a glorious, glorious experience! God spoke further to my spirit to let me know how much he loved the sister that was troubled. I was so thankful to God that he could use me to go the extra mile, so that he could make peace. There's no big or little, right or wrong, people. God wants us all to have a yielded spirit. Amen.

Blind Bartimaeus, needing a miracle, pushed through the crowd to Jesus.

Nothing's changed. Jesus is the same yesterday, today, and forever.

We are no well-kept secret. He knows us through and through. He watches everything we do. His eyesight is . . .

Twenty-Twenty

~~~~~~~~~~~~

Like a picture postcard, the road we were on was unique. It was only a two-lane highway, but it wound along beside the ocean. The day was beautiful: blue sky, lazy clouds. Everything was so alive—you could smell the ocean, almost taste it. Truly, this was God's country. Now and then we saw a ship off in the distance, or a fisherman pulling a lobster trap or running a line of equipment. Sometimes we saw white-capped waves crashing against the distant shore. A gospel tape played softly on our truck radio. As we rounded a long corner, we saw a string of cars that seemed to stretch on for three-quarters of a mile or more. Standing there was a man flagging us down. He said, "You'll have to stop here! A man has gone mad in the village. He's in the woods. He's got a shotgun and a rifle. He's taking potshots at just anyone."

It was early in the afternoon and already there were cars and trucks behind us. With our big rig, it was impossible to turn around. We had no alternative but to wait. The only thing we could do to help was to pray. We prayed, "Dear Lord, only you can cause this situation to end peacefully, without bloodshed." We prayed numerous times that the man would give himself up.

Darkness was closing in when a SWAT team consisting of several trucks, a van, dogs, and many SWAT team members—probably about twenty-five—arrived from Halifax with guns and all sorts of equipment. They looked like a small army! We prayed again, "Lord, do whatever you need to do to cause this to end peacefully." About that time, our sunny day ended, and a cold rain began. It rained and rained while the clock kept ticking. Hour after hour went by, until finally, about eleven o'clock, the man, so cold he was nearly freezing, walked out onto the highway with his hands up in the air as a sign of surrender. It was over. A bloodless victory. The highways were opened up again, and we went on.

In the wee hours of Sunday morning, we parked our trailer on the church lot and caught a few hours sleep in order to be ready for the morning service. We must always be at our best and ready to do our best for a God that is The Best!

We played our instruments and sang the songs of Zion. We preached that morning on how God had taken a blind beggar and opened his eyes. (See Mark 10:46-52.) We preached that God was still in the healing business and is still a surgeon; that he always could, and still does, operate without a knife. When we called for people to take a step of faith, to come forward for prayer and healing, there were only three who came. After praying for them, the service ended. We were scheduled to be in another town quite a few miles away that night, so we didn't dilly-dally. We got ready to leave as quickly as we could.

A lot of times we don't know what God has done, but we go on in faith. We're the little "i" in the middle of faith, and together with the Holy Spirit, we lift up Jesus. We must never take any credit when God heals, and we must never

blame ourselves if he doesn't. All we do is combine our
belief with theirs. It's their faith that will make them whole.
Later, when we received our mail, there was a special
letter in it. It was from one of the ladies who came forward
that morning. It read:

> Hello, there. I was finally able to get your address—I
> was beginning to give up hope. I wanted to share with you
> the healing I received when you were here. I was one of the
> three ladies who came up for healing. My vision was
> doubled; I had headaches and a pain in my eye. The retina
> was torn or tearing. I had an appointment to see a special-
> ist the next day—I'd seen him several times before, but I
> was told this time to bring a driver because my eye was
> going to be dilated. He told me that my eye was badly dete-
> riorated, and he said he didn't know what was causing it. A
> virus maybe? Well, I went to see him the next day, truly
> believing that I was healed. When I got to his office, the
> eye specialist dilated my eye. I could tell he was excited.
> He kept saying, 'This is hard to believe, this is hard to be-
> lieve. I will have to dilate the other eye.' Well, needless to
> say, he was surprised. His exact words were, 'Wow, it's re-
> ally healed. In fact, it's perfect!' He dropped into his chair
> and leaned back. His face showed that he was puzzled.
> 'It's a miracle, isn't it doctor?' He never said a word, but
> his eyes spoke volumes. I told him I wasn't surprised, be-
> cause I'd been to a healing service on Sunday. I went up front
> and I was prayed for. I believed the Lord Jesus healed my
> eye. He said, 'That's great. Your eyes are perfect! I'd like to
> see you next year around this time.' So an appointment was
> made for me to come back a year later. My brother and sister
> in Jesus, I'll never forget the words you said to the congrega-
> tion: that Jesus is a surgeon, that he is an eye-specialist, and
> many times his operating theater is around the altar. Just
> like Bartimaeus of old, my eyesight now is twenty-twenty.

In God's word it is written that old men see visions and young men dream dreams. (Joel 2:28, 29)

God still has His modern-day Josephs who, guided by the Holy Spirit, can interpret. (Gen. 41:15)

A Dream

~~~~~~~~~

My calling to the ministry came at thirteen thousand feet over the North Atlantic on a 747 jet; and Sister Annie's call came in our little restaurant where the Lord spoke to her through scripture, telling her to ". . . do the work of an evangelist" (2 Timothy 4:5).

Prior to stepping out in faith, we visited some of our longtime friends in the area where we lived. One couple was Reuben and Loretta. They lived in a country area and up a long hill. We decided that we would go say good-bye to them. What we didn't know was that a spring storm had hit the area and that the roads were white with about two inches of fresh snow. We made an attempt to drive up the hill but soon lost all traction and began spinning our wheels. We had a small car with all-season tires, but I guess the seasons did not include the spring snow! We would get only a short way up before having to back down. We tried it several times but couldn't get any distance up that hill.

So we did the only thing we knew to do when all else fails—we joined hands in the car and prayed, "Lord if you want us to visit Reuben and Loretta, you'll have to send an angel to push this car." (Thinking back, we chuckle as we recognize our childlike faith.) I said to Sister Annie, "One last attempt—hang on, we're off!" We tried once again. I don't know exactly what it was that made me take my foot off the accelerator, but I did. There are no words in man's vocabulary to properly explain the awesome presence that came into the vehicle. Annie looked at me and I at her. We could sense an unseen presence. I said very quietly, "Look," pointing down at my feet. "I'm not touching the accelerator." The car kept working it's way up the hill. It was a very steep, long hill. Finally, with neither one of us saying another word, there we were at the top!

Sister Loretta and Brother Reuben invited us into their home and said, "You're just in time for coffee." We shared with them that God had called us into the ministry and that we had come to say good-bye. While we were sitting there, Sister Loretta said, "Annie, I'm really perplexed about something. I wonder, if I share it with you, perhaps you can help me understand, because my spirit is troubled." She went on, "I had a dream last night about my mother. I dreamed that Jesus came, and he was in the house, but mother was outside picking flowers in the garden. I called to her, 'Mother, come in. Jesus is here.' My mother didn't want to come in. I was really troubled, because I know my mother was a God-fearing woman. I know that when she died, she went to heaven, so I couldn't understand why she wouldn't come and see Jesus. I called her several times, but she wouldn't even look up, even though she must have heard me." Loretta continued, "Sister Annie, why do you suppose my mother wouldn't come in?"

The Bible tells us that we must be instant in season. (See 2 Timothy 4:2.) Of course, I don't interpret dreams, but she had asked me a direct question, so in my heart I prayed, "Lord, help! You used Daniel to interpret King Darius's dreams. Please help me now, O Lord!"

I said to Loretta, "Well, Sister Loretta, it's this way—you said you know that your mother was a God-fearing woman, right?" She nodded. "You believe your mother is now in the presence of the Lord and the angels. Loretta nodded. Well, I believe the Lord confirmed that by her presence in your dream. But, Loretta, Jesus came to see you. He didn't come to see your mother because she's with him anyway." Loretta's face lit up as the truth hit home. She said, "Why yes, of course, that's it! He came to see me!" She said, "Thank you so much Sister Annie." I, in turn said, "Well, thank God."

A RING OF TRUTH

We fellowshipped for awhile, enjoying the presence of the Lord. Thinking back, to even say good-bye was a step of faith. We hadn't sold our place yet. We had all our belongings in our little car and that one wheel trailer.

Excusing herself, Loretta left the room briefly, returning shortly with her purse in hand. She opened it, then taking out a hundred dollar bill, she passed it to me. Up rose my pride! You see, Jerry and I had worked hard all of our lives. We didn't accept anything from anybody. No one gave us anything, and we were proud of that. She handed the hundred dollar bill to me, and I said, "No, Sister Loretta! We don't want it or need it. Our place is going to sell. God is going to supply our need. (See Phillipians 4:19.) We are going to be well taken care of."

She looked at me for awhile and then said, "Here Annie, take it!"

I said, "No, I can't Loretta. Put that money back in your purse. God is going to take care of us."

"Child," she said, "how do you think he's going to do it? Take this hundred dollar bill." There was a certain *ring of truth* in her statement, "how do you think he's going to do it?"

Learning to Receive

Finally I took it, and there I sat with a hundred dollar bill in my hand with no idea what to do with it! I sure didn't feel very good about it. I didn't know whether to put it in my pocket, or lay it on my Bible, or give it to Jerry. I was really uncomfortable with it. You see, I had not learned to *receive* yet. The Bible says that it is more blessed to give than receive. I could see she wasn't going to take it back, that much was clear. Finally she said, "Brother Jerry, it looks like Annie has a hundred dollar bill there, doesn't it!" Jerry said, "Well, yes, it looks that way."

"You better have one too," she said. In her hand was another hundred dollar bill. God was teaching us a lesson in humility—we were humbled that day, amen. After a final prayer, where we joined hands and hearts, praying one for another, then we left. The snow had melted away, and the roads were safe again. Soon we were back on the main highway. Annie looked at me, and I at her because God had proved himself. He had shown us, as only God can, that he was going to supply all our needs to go tell the good things that he has done for us, and to know that he, Jesus himself, is walking with us along this Miracle Road.

Sure, the Miracle Road has more than a few bumps, as you'll read in the next story. But, hey! It has so many blessings, it's hard to keep count. Today we're traveling down . . .

Highway 81 South

The last trace of daylight was fighting its losing battle with the shadows of night as we pointed our truck south over the bridge across the Susquehanna River at Harrisburg, Pennsylvania. I calculated the miles ahead and made a mental note to get started earlier tomorrow. North Carolina was still many miles off.

Coming off the Harrisburg Bridge, we began to climb a long upgrade. Our old truck started to slow down under the pressure of the pull. We were about two or three miles south of the river when we heard a strange sound, a grinding whine in the truck. It nearly blew our minds. Annie turned to me and asked in a nervous concerned voice, "What is it?"

"I don't know," I said, "but you're looking at a very worried man!" I edged the pickup and trailer over to the side of the highway. We had just made it there and were still going about twenty-five miles per hour when Annie spotted a tire zooming past her side of the truck.

"Jerry, a tire just went by my window."

"Annie, that's our tire," I said. We slowed down even more to about fifteen miles per hour when the second tire flew by. Talk about scary!

Annie said, "There goes another tire." Help, Lord!

HEAVENLY INSURANCE POLICY

Many times we have prayed for protection along the highways. Some people have prayed that angels be posted to help us in times of trouble. I believe they were on the job that night. Praise the Lord! Our truck and trailer came to a stop on the edge of Highway 81. Phew! We sat there in the cab and shook, thanking God. It didn't take long to find the trouble: our truck was a "duelly" with four rear tires. But now we had lost half of them. The two tires that had whizzed by Annie's window were indeed ours. The pavement bore a thin line where the axle had scuffed along for thirty feet or so. "Now what shall we do, Lord?"

The night was dark and cold. The only sign of life was a light in the distance. A house . . . people . . . a telephone, maybe? I said, "Annie, we'll get some help at that house. Come on, let's go." We walked, we crawled, we stumbled up an embankment toward the light. About half a mile later, we reached the driveway. It felt like we had trudged for miles. As we got closer to the house, Annie said, "Man, we escaped a bad accident. We could have died on that highway, but Jerry, these farmhouses have dogs, big dogs. Now we will get eaten by a dog."

We made it to the door, knocked, and a trembling female voice said, "Yeah, what do you want?" We explained our problem. She spoke to her father telling him there were two evangelists on his doorstep who needed help. He opened his door wide and invited us into his home. We shared with him what had happened.

"Surely, God has spared your lives!" he said excitedly. I glanced at his telephone. "Yes, go ahead and use the phone, by all means."

I opened the yellow pages to churches, because we needed someone honest to guide us to the right garage.

There were five full gospel churches listed. As I prayed about the one to call, a strange thing happened. One church name seemed to rise up from the book toward me. Instantly, I knew the number God wanted us to call, so I dialed. The voice that listened to my story said, "Where exactly are you? Okay! We'll be right there." They came, several men in trucks . . . cars . . . with cheerful voices . . . friendly faces.

"We'll need a wrecker," someone said.

"I know one," another responded. One phone call, and a few minutes later, the wrecker arrived. Our truck was disconnected and quickly in tow to a wrecking yard, the trailer left along the highway with flares burning.

A PRICELESS SOUL

Gordon, the junkyard owner, was a chain smoker. He'd puff one down to the butt, then he'd light another from it. He insisted that we come into his home to meet his wife, Martha, and to be out of the cold while our truck was being fixed. There were two other workers sitting there, a cloud of smoke above their heads as they matched their employer, puff for puff. Annie whispered to me, "What are we going to do?" I said, "We're going to do what we always do. We're going to lift up Jesus, amen."

The men worked, finding parts and installing them. Every time the wrecking yard owner, Gordon, looked at me, he seemed to almost ask a question but stopped short. About three o'clock in the morning, our old truck was again ready to go back on the highway and haul in the trailer.

Annie was left alone with Martha, the junkyard owner's wife. They sat facing a window where Martha had rigged a bare light bulb outside in a tree to watch wild animals. She left food for them each night. As they watched, a possum munched on something, then almost like a scene in a movie, the possum left, and a white-tailed deer walked in. Martha was overwhelmed with hurts from her past. Abused and tormented, she was a frightened little girl in a woman's body crying out, "Help, help . . . I'm at my wit's end."

Our God hears the cry of a hurting heart. Now I knew why our truck had broken down. This was no coincidence, this was God. Martha gave her heart to Jesus that night, and for sure, all heaven rejoiced. The lights of the truck and trailer shone in the driveway as Gordon and Jerry returned.

We caught a little sleep before morning came. After breakfast, Gordon finally asked his question. "Do you know how lucky you are?" He didn't wait for an answer. "I've seen many accidents like this. I get there most times just as the bodies are being removed. The truck turns left or right and the trailer goes through the truck cab. Do you know how lucky you are?"

"Sir, God looks after us," I said. I thought it was time to ask how much we owed. I was about to when I felt a holy nudge to go out to the trailer and bring in all five of our musical singing cassettes and give them to our new sister in the Lord, Martha.

We had another cup of coffee and waited for the subject of the bill to come up. I just knew it would be a large amount; after all, three men, all those parts, a large wrecker. Oh Lord, would Visa cover it? Finally I said, "Well, this is the part I like best." All eyes turned toward me. "Paying the bill." Without hesitation, Gordon spoke up and said, "Oh! There will be no bill. You people are disciples."

Thank you, Gordon; thank you, Martha; thank you, Jesus. We said good-bye and drove off down Highway 81 South.

We prayed before traveling Highway 81 South. Prayer activates God's protection policy. His salvation plan is based on "faith alive." His personal guarantee is that He has everything . . .

Under Control

〰〰〰〰

Needing directions, we stopped at the state welcome center where they proudly promoted the Wright brothers and their famous antique airplane, Kittyhawk. Above the information desk, a banner read: Welcome to North Carolina—First in Flight. They presented us with a state map asking, "Where y'all going?"

"Eden," we replied.

Picking up his liquid marking pencil, the attendant blazed a yellow trail across the map through a tangled web of Carolina roads. As we left, "Y'all come back," echoed in a southern twang behind us.

We followed the directions the welcome center attendant advised. Night caught us high in the Blue Ridge Mountains—no moon, no stars—it just had to be the darkest night that we'd ever seen. We were already headed down the mountain when we spotted the sign that read: 9% grade. Our truck lights reflected on yet another reminder that we had gone beyond the point of no return. All that the sign said was Lover's Leap, but that spoke volumes to us. Our hearts jumped into our mouths as we began our fight to hold back our heavy rig.

It pays to be prayed up. We were in big trouble. We needed supernatural assistance. If Jesus didn't help us, we knew that we would be in his presence any minute. Smoke had filled the cab of the truck. We could hardly breathe when we finally ground to a stop. We blocked the wheels, and it was then that we spotted the brake drums—they were white with heat! It took forty-five minutes for them to cool from white to red to a dull black.

Many miles later, our crippled truck crept into Eden with only its headlights working. From there we called an old friend who came quickly to our rescue.

"We've got no running lights, Grady," we said.

"Well, you'll never make it through Eden. There's police all over the place," he said. "Tell you what—I'll drive behind you with my four-way flashers on. That's all we can do." So we did just that, and, amen, we made it. Praise the Lord!

After we pulled into the church lot, Brother Grady said, "I thought you told me you had no running lights. They were on all the way through the city. Try them again," he said. I pulled on the light switch and everything remained dark. Once more he had met our need. (See Phillipians 4:19.)

The next day, our friend, Pastor Pete, decided to check out the damage and fix it. He owned a small construction company and had enough tools and equipment and know-how to be God's man of the hour. We backed the trailer over the pit to fully assess the damage. Broken springs, broken shackles. "It sure doesn't look good," said Pastor Pete. "We'll jack up the frame, then we'll know more." So we did, and with each click of the jack, the picture became clearer. All that held the trailer to the chassis was the weight.

Parts began to fall off into the pit as we rejoiced, giving
God the glory for sparing our lives.

We shared in a revival there that lasted for almost two
months. Night after night, God moved on hearts: saving
souls, restoring lives, and healing the sick. The Holy Spirit
was at work drawing those who would come to Jesus. One
night a man spotted the lighted sign out front while driving by. He glanced in, but he kept on going. He said that
several miles later, he felt an irresistible urge to return. So
he did, and he shared his testimony, blessing us with this
nugget from his treasury of memories.

"I had a close friend who was, in his own words, the
world's worst cusser. Every second word that he used was
profanity. He went to a full gospel revival one night and
was moved by the Holy Spirit to give his heart to Jesus.
Shortly after, he put out a sort of a fleece to God. He said,
'Lord, if you can clean up my cussing mouth, then I'll know
that you're real, and that my salvation is real.' Well, for a
God that rolled back the Red Sea, healed lepers, opened
blind eyes, fed multitudes with just two fishes and five
loaves, and even raised the dead, it's no great task for the
Holy Spirit to houseclean his new temples, so that's what
he did! And Colonel Sanders, the owner of the fried chicken
outlets worldwide, never cussed again. He served the Lord
faithfully until he graduated to glory."

With our trailer restored, we headed south to orange
country, the sunshine state of Florida, to hold meetings in
the Tampa Bay area. We sort of kept our eyes open for the
right trailer to replace ours. One day Annie decided to look
through an RV trailer magazine.

"Look, Jerry, here's exactly the trailer we've prayed
for. It's everything we've asked the Lord for—tri-axial,

forty-feet long, washer and dryer, a slide-out—the works! That's our trailer!"

"Hold on, Annie. I saw that trailer and decided, no, we can't afford a trailer like that. Besides, it's a private sale— what would we do with the trailer we've already got?"

"But Jerry, it says 'desperation sale—bank repossession.' You need to call them." So I did, and as I hung up the receiver I said, "We're going to go and have a look at the trailer, but don't get your hopes up."

"OK," Annie said, but in her heart she later confided that it was a done deal. We'd be living in that trailer soon.

"Yes, we like the trailer, but we have to trade in the one we have, you know. We have a thirty-five footer. It's over near Lakeland," we told the sales manager.

"Well," he said, "We have to go that way tomorrow. We'll take a look at it. Now, it's only fair to tell you that we've had other offers on the trailer, but no one has come up with the cash, and the bank is pushing us to get the money."

About that time, a still, small voice spoke to my inner man. "Write a check to bind the sale in the amount of half of what they're asking." I knew this was the Holy Spirit speaking to me, so I wrote the check, and he promised to see us the next day. In the morning, they came and looked ours over good.

"How's the roof?" they asked.

"Great. We just had it redone a short time ago."

"What about the floor?"

"Well, it's good. It's a solid floor," we assured them.

"OK, everything else can be fixed. You've got yourself a deal. Sign here." So we signed.

"Oh, by the way," he said, "yesterday after the bank accepted your offer, we had seven more, all for more than yours, much more." We knew that this was God. He had this trailer on hold just for us. Needless to say, without a hitch, the pieces fell together. When God's in it, it just cannot fail, amen.

Since then we never take anything for granted, especially road directions. We always ask, "Is that a road that the transport trucks use?" Tractor trailers always avoid steep mountain roads.

FOOTNOTE

God knows everything. We're not a well-kept secret to him. He heard our prayers and he saved our lives that day on Lover's Leap Mountain. He had help waiting in the valley to help us restore our broken vehicle. He heard our prayer for another trailer, and he supplied our need. Yes, God has everything under control!

He still saves,
He still heals,
He still delivers,
He never compromises,
He is consistently the same,
He is waiting to hear the
Cry of the captives.
All Hell flees
At his command.

Sister Freddie's Deliverance

〰〰〰

Hey! There's a real devil loose on planet earth! Sister Freddie had backslid again. Satan had a stronghold on her that she couldn't seem to break. Time and again she lost the battle as she plunged narcotics through the needle into her body. In a way, she reminded me of the man at the tombs mentioned in Mark 5. He was possessed by the devil (inhabited by an unclean spirit), but his inner man wanted to be set free so "when he saw Jesus afar off, he ran and worshipped him" (Mark 5:6). Just as Legion came to Jesus to be freed, Sister Freddie came to church, and to the altar, needing deliverance. She looked at me and began to cry great sobs, her shoulders shaking. I put my arms around her, and she laid her head on my shoulder. She cried and cried. After a while I said, "Are you ready for me to pray for you now?" She said, "Yes, please pray for me."

As I prayed for her, she went down in a crumpled heap on the floor. She lay there while I began praying with others. I don't know what it was that caused me to glance at her, but as I did, she sat straight up with her hands curled like animal claws. She was looking into my face with such hatred that I knew the evil spirits had manifested. I walked over to her, placed my hand on her head, and she fell back down again. The ushers ran to get cloths to mop her brow because by then she had begun to sweat. Her blouse became askew as she writhed on the floor. Froth bubbled from her mouth. Hell was having a field day within Sister Freddie. The Bible says, "take authority" (Luke 9:11). We did just that—we began to rebuke the devil and bind the evil spirits.

TOTAL AUTHORITY

The pastor was at the pulpit, watching what was happening. He came down and began to pray for her. She put out one frail arm, and the evil thing in her threw the pastor right across the pew. Sister Freddie weighed, perhaps, 110 pounds, and the pastor who at about 230 pounds, was not a small man! He said, "Sister Annie, Sister Freddie's been on drugs." So we continued to pray and to take authority in Jesus' name. We ordered the demon of narcotics to come out of her in the name of Jesus. Standing firmly on the rock of Christ Jesus, we took total authority until the shaking and writhing finally stopped. A look of peace came over her. Then the pastor and the congregation began to sing, "Peace, peace, wonderful peace; coming down from the Father above. Sweep over my spirit." I believe God's peace swept over Sister Freddie's spirit that night.

Sister Freddie left the service, free from Satanic oppression, praise God! He whom the Son sets free is free indeed!

FOOTNOTE

Every spiritual prison has a scriptural key! Feel free to write us sharing your need. We'll pray for you. Our address is in the back pages of this book.

Jerry and Annie.

Man and medicine have accomplished much. But many times they are forced to admit there's no cure known to mankind.

It's at those times that God moves in power of authority, so whatever we do we must never tire of praying. Some say the squeaky wheel gets the grease, so never, never, never . . .

Stop Praying

~~~~~~~~~~

Spring is refreshingly special: everything's alive, ready to bud, blossom, or bloom, including young love. You can hear it in their voices and see it in their faces. Everything about them says, "Hey! Look at us! We're in love!"

Mindy was the only daughter of Pastor Roy. She was a little snip of a thing, head-over-heels in love with Mike. He made no secret that his search for love had ended with his Mindy. Mike was working at Burger King for the summer holidays, so Mindy got a job there, too. Mindy's mother said, "Mindy only got the job at Burger King so that she can look at Mike!" There was never a question of 'if.' The only unknown factor was 'when' they would put God's holy stamp of approval on their lives. Every time we saw them they would say, "We want you to be at our wedding."

Being invited to a wedding is always a blessing for us, but most of the time we're too far away to go. When Mike and Mindy said "I do," we were several states away in Mississippi. Sometime later, we received a request from Mike and Mindy to visit them. It seemed they both wanted to have a child but had become quite concerned because nothing had happened, so they consulted their doctor. He ran a series of examinations on them both. The final results were that Mindy had endometriosis.

"You have a disease that makes it impossible to carry a child," the doctor informed her. "But you do have other options, such as adoption, and you're young, so you have plenty of time."

ANOTHER OPTION

There's a Bible verse that says, "Oh, I know who I have believed in, and I am persuaded that He is able to keep that which I've committed unto him against that day." Mindy had one option that the doctors never mentioned. Being a pastor's daughter, Mindy had seen God heal many times. She was born again and therefore entitled to a healing from the Great Physician. So she opted for prayer. Prayer is the key to God's mighty hand. The Bible says, "The effectual, fervent prayer of a righteous man availeth much" (James 5:16). God heard their prayer, and he responded—Mindy became pregnant! She gave birth to a healthy, beautiful baby girl. Praise the Lord! There's a gospel song of victory entitled, "He'll Do It Again." He did. About a year later, Mindy became pregnant again. She delivered another healthy baby girl. He'll do it again, amen. He did it again twelve months later: another baby girl.

Shortly after, Mike and Mindy sent us this message: "Please, please, please, stop praying!"

He healed every sickness and every disease as he ministered to multitudes along Galilee's shore.

Take heart, he still ministers to those who reach out to him. There's nothing he cannot heal; he even has . . .

A Cure for AIDS

≈≈≈≈≈≈≈

The same Jesus that raised the dead, healed the lepers, and who did so many other wonderful things, said that he would send another Comforter (John 14:16), and that far greater things would be done in his name.

We were in church one night when a lady from the congregation came to me and said, "Sister Annie, Pastor Lowery and his wife are going down to Nashville to visit my brother tomorrow. He's in the hospital. Would you come along and pray for him?" I said, "Well, sure, Sister Maxine, I'd love to." Shortly after, the pastor's wife, Abby, took me aside to tell me, "Sister Annie, her brother is HIV positive, and he's in the last stages."

As I had promised, I was ready to travel when the car's horn honked. As I got into the car, I told the pastor, his wife, and Maxine, "Jerry couldn't go. He's catching up on some things. Jerry said, 'You go for both of us.' So here I am."

Traveling along the highway, they informed me what lay ahead. It seems the pastor had led Maxine's brother to the Lord a few weeks before. It turned out the pastor was going to the hospital to help this AIDS victim get his affairs in order. They were about to transfer him from that hospital to an institution for the terminally ill. When we got there, he was in the solarium section, seated in a chair. They introduced him to me. "Sister Annie," they said, "meet Maxine's brother, John."

"Hello, John. So glad to meet you," I said. As I did, I sized John up. He was a tall man, so tall that the chair he sat in looked much too small for him. He had lost most of his body weight. That was the way the disease had manifested itself in him during the last stages. Plus, his hands bothered him. We talked awhile, and then his sister wheeled him back into the hospital room where the nurse helped him back on to his bed.

He looked so pitiful sitting there on the bed. My eyes kept focusing on his hands. I don't know what he had on his hands, but they were covered with some kind of bulky bandage wrapping to protect them. He couldn't eat with a spoon, couldn't use a fork; he couldn't even hold a pen to write a letter. He couldn't do anything. Even the air hurt his hands, they were so sensitive.

Look Through My Eyes

We prayed for him again before leaving. As we were walking away, he was sitting on the bed waving good-bye. It was then that the Holy Spirit bid me to stop and turn around and have one last look, only this time, through the eyes of Jesus. So I did. I stopped and turned around to look at him once more. The Bible says that Jesus looked on the multitude with compassion (Matthew 14:14).

If you look through the eyes of compassion that God has given you, you'll be looking through eyes of love. The still, small voice of God began to echo, "Now, go pray for him." I turned and went back and said, "Brother, can I pray for your hands?" As he looked at me, even his eyes seemed to be hurting. Then because his hand were so sensitive, he carefully placed them in mine. I just prayed a simple prayer.

It didn't matter that the man had AIDS. It wasn't important how he had gotten it. All that mattered was that I obey God and pray with all my heart, and believe not just with my head, *hoping*, but with my heart, *believing*!

Jerry and I then went south to Texas to minister along the Mexico-United Sates border until the warm spring winds prompted us to turn back north. On the way back, we stopped again at Sister Maxine's church.

HE'S HEALED

It was during a mid-week service. I was already ministering around the altar when Sister Maxine came in, and she spotted me right away. She excitedly half yelled "Sister! Sister Annie! My brother's healed! Praise God, my brother is healed. Hallelujah!"

She caught me by surprise. All I could think of was that maybe his hands are healed. I said, "Wonderful, praise the Lord! He's got those old bandages off his hands." She said, "No, you don't understand. He is healed. Praise God! 100% healed!" She began to shout, "He's healed! He's healed! Praise God!" Then she asked, "Are you going to be here Wednesday night?"

"Yes, we will," I said.

"Good. He'll be wanting to see you," Maxine said.

What a transformation! When he came walking in, I almost didn't recognize him. He had regained most of his body weight. The first thing he did when he saw me was raise his hands above his head.

He entered the sanctuary just as the Bible says, "Enter into his gates with thanksgiving, and into his courts with praise . . . " (Psalm 100:4). His healing testimony didn't stay within the walls of the church. In the service that night, there was a pew filled with his relatives who had come to Christ because of his powerful healing testimony. New babes in the Lord, hallelujah. There is nothing impossible with God!

That's what it's all about, friends. Everything God does for you is to bring the lost to him. God loves us and wants to heal us, but his main concern is *the lost* coming to Christ.

It's true. The Bible reads: "I wish above all things that thou mayest prosper and be in health, even as thy soul prospereth" (3 John 2). If your soul prospers, praise God. That will speak to the hurting people who are without Christ. Soul prosperity means a holy well-spring of abundance from which you can draw an endless supply of refreshing, living water! This well-spring entices many unsaved to taste and see that God is good.

Yes, God is good, and, yes, God has a sure cure for AIDS. And he'll use whomever he heals of any sickness or affliction for his glory. The question is, are you ready to be used by God?

FOOTNOTE

For those who are suffering from AIDS: yes, there's a cure for AIDS. It doesn't matter how you got it. You can be healed if your heart is right with God. God hates the sin, not the sinner. You must give your heart to Jesus. Not just your head, but also your heart. Then, as a repentant child of God, you are eligible for his healing touch. It's all in his heavenly insurance policy, called "Salvation." Amen.

Our God will make a way through the mountain if we can't get over the top. There's one thing I've leaned about our Heavenly Father: His mercy and love never stop. His promise still holds true: salvation, healing and . . .

Deliverance

〰〰〰〰

A spectacular crimson sunset disappeared behind Virginia's rolling hills. "Beautiful day tomorrow," Annie said, as if she was reading my thoughts. She continued, "There's a lot of traffic tied up behind us, Jerry—must be fifteen or twenty cars! Maybe we should pull over and let them pass."

An automotive service center came into view just as she finished speaking.

"Yes, I know," I told her. "We'll stop for fuel at that Shell station."

"Bad mistake," I said out loud as I pulled off the road just before the gas station. "Oh well, we'll get turned around at the first wide spot." The road dwindled down until it was just wide enough for one vehicle, then abruptly came to an end. Sizing up the situation, we spotted a place large enough for us to turn, but a car was blocking the entrance.

"Hope they're home," I thought, as I walked to the door and sounded the doorbell. "I'll ask them to move their car." I rang and waited, then rang again, but there was nothing but silence from within. As I walked away, I decided to try another house nearby.

A young man quickly responded at the door and to the questions I had for him as well.

"Oh, those people in the white house—they're gone to an auction," he said. "They'll be home around midnight, but, hey, if all you want to do is turn, my grandmother lives just up the hill right there." He pointed to a house almost hidden by trees with a narrow driveway and a steep, deep cliff on one side. It looked threatening!

"There is room for you to turn around in the yard," he said.

"Hold on Jerry, you can't take this rig up that hill!" Annie half-way yelled.

"There's no other way. You wait here," I instructed her. But, no, she climbed into the cab, gave me a determined look, and with her voice putting words to her facial expression, "I go where you go, Jerry," she said.

Up that narrow drive we went as the Spirit of the Lord guided us into the back yard. It was then that things went from bad to worse. A loud, angry screaming voice, "You . . . . you dirty rotten . . . ! Who do you think you are? What do you think you're doing? Where do you think you're going? This is my property! You have no right to be here!" As he got closer, we noticed he smelled even worse than he sounded. That old demon of alcohol had full control of him. We knew we were dealing with a man drunk out of his mind. He slurred again, and snarled, "I ought to get my gun and blow your brains out!"

We prayed, "Help us Lord, help us!" Just a simple prayer, an SOS to Jesus. Annie spoke and said, "Please sir, we just need to turn around and get back on the highway." But her words seemed to fall on deaf ears.

"Who are ya?" he said. "Let me see your driver's license."
He snarled again as he read our Canadian driver's licenses.

"Why, you're not even from this country. You're aliens!
I oughtta blow your brains out!"

We knew full well that it wouldn't take him long to get
a gun. His threat, fueled with alcohol, could cause him to
squeeze the trigger. Both of us began to bind the devil without saying one word out loud. God's Word reads: ". . . if any
two of you shall agree on earth as touching any thing that
they shall ask, it shall be done for them of my Father which
is in heaven" (Matthew 18:19).

CALL ON THE LORD

"Help, Lord!" I was praying and crying out to the Lord
to speak to my spirit. Sister Annie said, "This is not a good
situation, Lord. A gun, alcohol, and a raging madman."

Our God moves in mysterious ways, his wonders to
perform. All of a sudden, we heard a shaky voice from one
of the windows.

"What's going on out there?" A little gray-haired woman
peered out, trying to see what the commotion was. Without hesitation I told her, "My husband and I have made a
wrong turn off the highway. This was the only place that
we could turn around. Your nice, considerate son is trying
to help us."

"That's right, Ma," her son said. "I'm helping them turn
around. Back up, buddy, turn sharp, cut your wheels—a
little to the left." Suddenly we backed over his concrete
well cover.

"No problem," he laughed. "Don't worry about that—
it's only an old well cover."

Finally, yes, finally, we were turned and ready to go down the driveway, which he still had blocked with his pickup truck.

"I'll walk down in front of you and move it." Then almost instantly, he changed his mind, and said, "Oh, no. You'll run me down." So he walked beside me behind the trailer. It was then that the old alcohol demon decided to raise its ugly head again.

"Canadians are no good!" he snarled. I shuddered. Oh no, not again. Then I sensed the still, small voice again, 'Just agree with him, just agree.'"

"You two," he went on, "are the stupidest people I've ever met."

I said, "Yup, we're not very bright."

"Why, I ought to call the police," he slurred.

"Good idea, call the police. That's a great idea," I agreed.

"Nah, they're even more stupid than you two. Go on, get a'going."

He moved his pickup truck and we pulled away. Our thought was, *Truck, don't fail us now!*

Thank you, Lord, for deliverance!

It's true. The effectual, fervent prayer of the righteous availeth much.

A Holy Spirit-filled temple is . . .

Totally A-Glow

We'd been detained in Tennessee, so we knew as we drove north towards Nova Scotia that we needed to keep a heavy foot on the gas pedal and a steady hand on the steering wheel to make a ladies' meeting where I was scheduled to minister. I considered phoning to cancel but could not bring myself to, thinking, where would they ever find another speaker in such short notice? I had been raised to believe persons are only as good as their word.

"Don't worry, Annie, we'll make it," Jerry said as we crossed the USA-Canada border, and sure enough, make it we did with only a few hours to spare.

"I just feel that something good is about to happen, I just know that something good is on its way . . . ."

From the second I walked into the conference room at the motel, I sensed the anointing of the Holy Spirit. These women were prayed up. They'd come expecting God to move. As they sang praising Jesus, every voice was united. "Come Holy Spirit, we need thee. Come Holy Spirit, we pray." Amen. He came sweeping in with power and authority.

The Holy Spirit loves to be with people as they lift up Jesus. So together we lifted up the Savior and the scripture came to life. He said, "And I, if I be lifted up from the earth, will draw all men to me" (John 12:32).

Some women stood on their feet only to fall in the Spirit; some to the floor, others across chairs. A little taste of heaven was happening at this Women Aglow meeting.

Then the healings started. Louise, a little French woman, came to me and said, "Sister Annie, I have a real problem with allergies. My nose is always running. It's driving me crazy. I get headaches and my eyes burn and itch; they're always weepy. I've tried doctors, but their medication doesn't help! I'm always miserable. Would you pray that Jesus will heal me?"

I took her hand, we prayed together, and Louise fell to the floor as the power of God hit her.

Another lady came to me and said, "Please agree with me in prayer. I'm having so much trouble with my son. The doctors said he has Attention Deficit Disorder. His school teachers don't know how to handle him, he's hyperactive, and the medication, Ritalin, has bad side effects. I want to stand in for my son."

"Sister, there's a scripture," I told her. "It's, 'He sent his word, and healed them . . . '" (Psalms 107:20).

I sensed in my spirit that the second she surrendered everything to God, there was a miracle in the making.

One woman wanted to be baptized in the Holy Spirit. She was a Mennonite lady who came dressed in their custom attire. With her hands lifted up to God, we prayed for her. Almost instantly it happened. "Here's my cup, Lord. I lift it up, Lord—come and fill this thirsting of my soul." And God did—he filled her with a new heavenly language that flowed from her trembling lips.

Sometime later, at another meeting, a lady hurried up to me with tears running down her face.

"Remember me, Sister Annie? You prayed for me at the Aglow meeting. My son had Attention Deficit Disorder, remember? Well, he's healed! His teachers want to know what's happened! He's totally healed! No more medication, he's healed!"

Then, while walking through a shopping mall, I heard a voice with an excited French accent call out, "Sister Annie!" It was Louise.

"I'm still healed! I'm still healed!" Her face reflected her inner condition. She indeed was totally "aglow"!

Now and then through life, we meet a giant. John, although just over five feet tall, was a giant in Jesus, indeed. Let me introduce you to . . .

Captain John

In evaluating our treasure chest of blessings, Sea Captain John was without a doubt a gem we prized highly. A special, special man who had traveled the entire world on sailing vessels. He had worked his way up from a cabin boy to able-bodied seaman then, eventually, captain. He had seen the heyday of sails and many years of steam sailing. There was something uniquely different about him, something extra special that we never could quite place our finger on. Later on, we found out that John was a Christian. Not an overly vocal, pushy one, but as sure as a steady hand on the helm keeps the ship on a straight course—John's compass was set for heaven's harbor.

STEADY AS SHE GOES

We were not back in town long before we were informed that John was sick unto death. It hurt us to hear that the Captain had fallen sick. We were told it was cancer. We went to see him and found him lying in bed, a shadow of his former self. We talked awhile, the Captain sharing with us his love of the Lord.

"I found Jesus many years ago," he confided. "I've served him on land and sea ever since."

No question about it, John was a born-again Christian who loved Jesus with all his heart. But cancer is no respecter of people. It had reduced him to just a shadow of his former self. He was now lying in bed in pain, so thin the skin barely covered those old bones. He had suffered much, this old sea captain. Once he had walked the rolling decks of tall ships, telling his crew in his gruff voice to put on more sail, to "hold her steady as she goes." Now this old salt lay without enough strength to rise from his bed of affliction. And, yet, at even the slightest mention of Jesus, an inner light brightened up his weathered face. I said, "Captain John, Jesus can heal you."

"Yes, my son," he said, "but if it's all the same to you I just want to go home. I just want to go home." I said, "Well, OK, Captain, but I could pray that Jesus would take that pain away from your body."

POWER IN PRAYER

"Go ahead, Jerry, my son, pray." So I knelt down beside the bed and laid my hands on his bony knees and began to pray. "Oh Father in heaven, look down on us today, and see your little child, Captain John, the sea captain. Lord, one more time, for your glory, please place your hand of healing on him." Suddenly, the pain was completely gone from Captain John's body. Oh! He's a God that can. He loves us little children no matter what age we are. Amen.

The next day, Captain John was feeling so good that they sat him outside the house to enjoy the beautiful sunshine. Some of his old lifetime friends came by to sit and talk to him. One of those friends dropped in to share the good news with us.

"You should see Captain John," he said. "What a transformation! Yesterday he looked liked death warmed over. Today, he's bright-eyed and chipper! It looks like he's going to make it." I turned to him and said, "No, we are going to bury John on the first day of the week."

ANCHORED IN JESUS

On Sunday, the first day of the week, Sister Annie and I were ministering at a church about a hundred miles away. We could not get back for his funeral, but Captain John wouldn't have wanted us to. That day, many gave their hearts to Jesus as Captain John's body was going below the sod. This thought engulfed me: his soul has taken it's last voyage, he's gone across the seas of eternity, his vessel blown along by the winds of the spirit, right up to heaven's harbor. I imagined him surrendering his earthly sea captainship papers to the mighty captain of them all, Captain Jesus. Hallelujah! He's anchored in the rock of ages, amen.

Total dominion, that's God's promise to us.

> Over the animals of the forest,
> Over the birds of the air,
> Over the fish of the ocean,
> Including . . .

Haddock at Ten O'Clock

※※※

Some of our greatest blessings happened in remote areas, such as the time we ministered in a little fishing village far off the beaten track in Nova Scotia. Revival had come after a long season of prayer. The Bible reads: "If my people, which are called by my name, shall humble themselves, and pray, and seek my face, and turn from their wicked ways, then I will hear from heaven, and forgive their sin . . ." (2 Chronicles 7:14). That's God's own word! He must therefore honor it. Since he's a God that backs up his word with action, people were being saved and healed, everything that could happen was happening.

This was a fishing area, and we love fish, so I said to one of the fishermen whom I knew by name, "Brother Dick, we would love to have some haddock. As you know, we're going south soon. We'd consider it a great blessing to have our freezer full of fish. We'll gladly pay whatever you ask." He said, "I'd like to help you, Brother Jerry, but I'm sorry to say we're not getting any haddock. We are catching some codfish, if that would be all right?"

I thought for a moment of how God had used a whale to transport Jonah to Nineveh, so I figured, well, he could cause a fish to bite a hook. I said, "I'm going to pray, Brother Dick, throughout the night. When ten o'clock comes tomorrow morning, you'll catch haddock."

When morning came, our fishing friend and his co-worker left the dock very early. Long before daylight, they were dropping in their baited hooks.

I wrote a song about a fisherman that went like this:

> Up in the morning before the sun rises,
> Still half asleep as I walk to the shore.
> The roar of the waves, the smell of the ocean,
> Makes me look up to heaven and thank the Lord.
> I climb on the boat and check the equipment
> And whistle a tune as I glance at the land.
> Then I let go the lines and pull back the throttle,
> Head out to sea—I'm a fisherman.

They had caught only codfish, no haddock, and it was now close to ten o'clock. They glanced at each other with a questioning look. "Getting near ten. Is there going to be any haddock?" Then it happened, the haddock arrived! It was as if God smiled and said, "Haddock you want, haddock you get." Dick brought up a haddock, then the man with him caught another. So it went for quite some time; every fish they caught was a haddock! Then, as suddenly as it started, it stopped, amen. Dick's face shone as he presented us with God's gift. They had even filleted them for us on the way back to shore. There was approximately forty-five pounds of beautiful fresh haddock fillets! Just enough to fill our freezer!

That winter, as we ministered from place to place through the southern United States, we often counted our blessings. Amen, blessed we were. We had haddock enough to share with others as we traveled on the Miracle Road for Jesus!

God is good!

Before leaving in clouds of glory, Jesus said he would send another Comforter, and far greater things would be done in his name. He said this . . .

I Promise You

———≈≈≈≈———

God just seems to bless in our services! We know that it's because of pre-prayers. We always invite the Holy Spirit to come, and together we uplift our mutual friend, Jesus, who said, "And I, if I be lifted up from the earth, I will draw all men to me" (John 12:32).

We're just simple folks; it amazes us every time God uses us. His Word in 1 Corinthians 1:27 states: "But God hath chosen the foolish things of the world to confound the wise. . ."

Springtime and sinus problems travel together as buddies—watery eyes, sneezing, running noses—the whole nine yards comes to life as winter surrenders to buds and blossoms. In a meeting, a lady came asking for prayer for her sinuses. She had some kind of a blockage. She told us her name was Francis. I spoke to her for a moment, then she shared her condition. She needed a touch from Jesus. We began to seek God for Francis. She was in a lot of pain. Sinus trouble and blockage can cause so much pain. We prayed for her around the altar that night, and I found myself saying something I've never said to anyone before, and I don't re-member saying it since. I found myself saying, "I promise you that God has healed you, I promise you, I promise you." It bubbled up from within me, from my spirit man, so I knew without question that this was a word of knowledge. I knew that God was about to heal her, but it didn't happen in that instant. When Francis went home, she was still in pain. She went to bed that night in more pain than she'd been in for a long time. Francis said that throughout the night the pain was so bad that it woke her up. My words echoed through her mind, "I promise you God has healed you!"

"So I got up and went to my kitchen, and something in my nose broke free," she said. "It began to run; it was to-tally free. Whatever was blocking my sinus had let go. Praise God, he's healed me!"

Amen, yes, he healed her because he's always the same—today, yesterday, tomorrow and forever, hallelujah! This I promise you, amen.

It has been said, the squeaky wheel gets the grease. So if at first your prayer is not answered, pray again. God sees all, hears all. He's no respecter of persons. Prayer will work for you; it worked for Brother . . .

Jonas

=〜〜〜〜〜=

When we received the call to come minister in several remote northern cities and towns, we never dreamed of the conditions that we would encounter.

We soon found out that Canada has a third world country living within it. It lies north of the sixtieth parallel. The airplanes that flew us from area to area were sixteen- to twenty-passenger types—too shaky for us to feel confident or even half-safe in—like a ramshackle building that time had ravaged, these planes had far exceeded their life expectancy.

In one of these northern meetings we met Jonas, a little Inuit man who had lived most of his life in the Goose Bay-Labrador area. As each service comes to a close, we always call for people that need prayer to come forward, and Jonas quickly came to the altar. He was full of arthritis. We prayed for him, telling him and everyone else there, "You know, we cannot heal anyone. Your pastor can't heal anyone. We can't heal you. Only the Lord can heal you. The doctors, if they're really honest, will tell you right up front that they can't heal you, either. *Only God can heal you." So we prayed for Jonas.*

We held services every night, and Jonas never missed one. Every service he was there, always wanting to be prayed for. Jonas was at the outdoor services on the native reservation as well as at the jail services, and, well, just about anywhere we turned, there was Jonas. He was like a little puppy. No, perhaps more like a shadow. Jonas was always there. The last night of our meetings finally came, and we were at the mother church in the area. The main service was over. The altar service time had begun, and Jonas hadn't yet received his healing. There he was again, following me. I'd walk away, then turn around. Yes, you're right, Jonas was there!

It was a powerful altar service. Perhaps 200 people came forward to receive of God. There was a beautiful move of God in the north country that night. God is everywhere. You can't go far enough north, or east, or south, or west to outrun him. He is just there; he's everywhere.

But the first man that wanted prayer that night was Jonas. I'd been praying for him all week. So I thought, "That should be enough. I've done my part, Lord. I've prayed and prayed for Jonas, time and again." So I went on to someone else to pray for them. But the Lord kept speaking to my spirit, saying, "Go pray for Jonas." About three times, maybe more, he told me, "Go back and pray for Jonas." Finally I said, "All right, Lord," and I did. In fact, I laid hands on him and prayed, casting the demon of arthritis right out of him. In that prayer, in that final prayer for Jonas, he was totally healed!

Later, Brother Jonas wrote us a letter that we still have. He told us he was able to go back out into the barren land—there's a lot of barren land up there in Labrador—to pick the red berries (they're something like cranberries). The letter arrived about a month after we'd left his area.

Jonas knew that Sister Annie didn't like flying at any speed. She'd told everyone that she hated flying. (As we mentioned before, those old planes were tissue thin. We could see outside in places that we shouldn't have been able to. Once they flew us in a hospital plane, and when it landed, the doors flew open by themselves. The runways were unpaved, short, full of rocks and potholes. But, praise the Lord, they had good pilots.) In his letter, Jonas had enclosed for us four little snowshoes he had made. He said the next time we came to Labrador, we could come on snowshoes since Sister Annie didn't like to fly.

He was totally healed. Praise the Lord!

FOOTNOTE

Jonas was like a squeaky wheel—determined to get God's attention. He did and was totally healed! God's timetable may have you scheduled for healing at the next altar service!

Rise and be healed in the name of Jesus!

The Holy Spirit is always prompting us to plant seeds of love and victory. We must dig out the bitter roots of doubt and . . .

Unbelief

~~~~~~~~~~~

One night after service, we accepted an invitation from a sister in the church to come to her house for a cup of coffee. We didn't know until we got there that she had another motive. Her husband was her reason; he was unsaved. We talked to him, and he quickly told us that our being in his home was his wife's idea, not his.

"I'm not part of that church," he added. His wife, who was standing close by, spoke. "Tell them about your ulcerated stomach." He didn't say anything, so she continued talking about how he had suffered with ulcers for more than twenty years. He was scheduled for an operation that week. I said, "Look, I'll pray for you if you'll let me. God heals that type of thing, you know. You could receive your healing." With all the people around, and his wife right there, he could hardly say no, so he nodded his consent. I asked his name and watched his lips move but couldn't make out what he said.

"My name is Jerry," I told him. "I'm a minister. God sometimes uses me in healing." I reached out, just barely touching him. Truth is, I felt an anti-spirit, but I prayed that God would heal his stomach and prove himself to him. After the prayer, he informed me that he was flying to the city where they would operate on him later in the week. I told him, "Go ahead. Keep your appointments. Go to the hospital, but before you have an operation, ask the doctors to re-examine you. God is in the healing business, and you've been prayed for. I believe that you're healed."

"Look," he said in a whisper, "I let you pray for me to keep my wife happy. I don't believe any of this foolishness."

Days later, he flew to the city for his operation. He never said a word about being prayed for because faith for him lay in the arm of flesh! The day of his operation came. They cut him open and could find absolutely no trace of ulcers. They informed him, "You're 100% well. Your ulcers have disappeared. We don't know how but they are gone."

God's word in Hebrews 3:12, mentions an evil heart of unbelief. There will be no unbelievers in heaven. I'd like to have been a mouse in the corner of his mind on his flight home. Ulcers of twenty years had disappeared! Prayer is the key to God's mighty healing power. Prayer unlocks the prison of unbelief.

What a Savior!

It's OK to give God the honor, the glory, the praise. It's OK to say, "I love you Jesus," and praise the Lord like our friend . . .

The Hallelujah Man

He looked me straight in the eye and said, "Brother Shaw, can Jesus heal a curvature of the spine?" Without even a second's pause, I said, "Absolutely! Jesus can heal anything." So I laid hands on him, and I prayed in faith, believing that God would straighten his spine. (See James 5:15.) I just knew in my spirit that God had healed him, and by the look on his face, he knew it, too. (See Matthew 9:22.)

After the service, a man and his wife asked if we would come minister at the senior-citizen home they managed about thirty-five or forty miles from where we were. I said we would, but our old truck was giving us difficulty. They said, "If we found a car for you, would you come?" I said of course we would. The next morning a brand new Lincoln Town Car sat ready and waiting for us to use. So we took off in a new car to the senior-citizen home to play our instruments, sing, preach, and testify, "go and tell the good things that I have done for thee." That's what the Lord told us to do—"Preach the word; be instant in season . . . " (2 Timothy 4:2). Pray and ". . . lay hands on the sick . . . " (Mark 16:18). ". . . do the work of an evangelist, make full proof of thy ministry" (2 Timothy 4:5). You can be afflicted with any sickness known to mankind and still go to heaven if you're saved; the bottom line is salvation. Jesus said to Nicodemus, "Ye must be born again . . . " (John 3:7). We pulled no punches at the seniors' home. Jesus himself said in John 8:32, "And ye shall know the truth, and the truth shall make you free." At the altar call, between twenty and twenty-five people made a first-time commitment to Jesus.

When we got back to the trailer, we saw a note taped to the door. Someone had come along, written a note, and taped it there for us (and for anyone else who'd come by) to read: "I have been to my doctor and had him check the curvature of my spine. He couldn't find it. It's gone, praise the Lord! I went to work at the logging mill after that. We generally handle a thousand logs a day, but because their supply was short, I had to work an extra shift. We handled in excess of two thousand logs that day. My back is still giving me no trouble whatsoever. Oh, hallelujah, I am healed!"

Hallelujah!

While ministering through Ontario, we stopped to visit with David and Norma Jean Mainse. They host the international television program *100 Huntley Street.*

We testified and sang our "Good Morning, Holy Spirit" song. Reverend Mainse shared with us that the program touches millions of lives daily. Praise the Lord.

Then, led by the Spirit, we blazed a trail of Holy Ghost meetings across Ontario with salvations and healings at every service.

HE DIRECTS OUR PATH

We continued on passing the many Indian Reservations of the Mohawk Tribe, once a powerful nation, now reduced to a shadow of their colorful past.

Then on to Winnipeg to minister with Reverend Willard and Betty Thiessen. They co-host *It's a New Day*, a life-changing television program.

Our next stop was at a native camp meeting north of the 60th parallel. Buckle up for another blessing . . .

The Gospel "Pill"

Y ou are now north of the 60th parallel" the sign said. We pushed on toward the Great Slave Lake and the town of Hay River.

We'd received the call to minister in the Northwest Territories about a year before and counted it a privilege to share at native camp meetings. (See Mark 16:15.) We knew that the church had prayed in faith, believing for souls to be saved and for miracles to happen. Upon our arrival, we talked with the pastor and his wife. Their expectations were high; they knew in their spirit that a powerful move of God was about to happen.

A few days later, early in the morning, I was putting some clothes on the line when I saw a young man moving very painfully towards me. I knew he was coming to talk to me. As he made his way toward me, I remarked that the weather was good. He nodded yes, then said, "I've been hearing about the camp meeting at Sandy Creek. I desperately need a healing, but I can't get there. I would like to go but the road is too bumpy and too long. I'm in excruciating pain."

At a quick glance I could tell that he was indeed in pain. He introduced himself as Rick, and said, "You're Sister Annie?" I assured him I was!

Jerry wasn't up yet because we were getting home every night after one o'clock, sometimes later. I wanted to pray for Rick, but I felt it would be best if Jerry and I prayed for him together. I didn't want to say to Rick, "Jerry's not up and around yet, would you mind coming back later?" I would have loved to have prayed for him and watched God heal his pain right there, but I knew all too well that God has an appointed time. All I could do was ask him to come back later. "Anytime after lunch will be just great, Rick. See you then!" I almost felt his pain as he made his way to his car which was parked beside the clinic.

Later in the afternoon, he came back. This time we were expecting him. We had prayed before he arrived.

It was no small task for him—it took everything he had to climb up the steps into the trailer. I said, "Rick, why don't you take this comfortable seat?" He slowly eased himself into the chair; we could see it even hurt for him to sit down.

"I'm a marine engineer. I hurt myself and my back is a mess. The doctors haven't helped. They're talking about an operation, but I believe the Lord will heal me. I've come for prayer."

My husband, Jerry, said, "Well, Rick, stand up then."

"Ouch!" I thought. I felt that was a mean thing to do because Rick was in so much pain. Again my husband told him, "Stand up, Rick." As he pulled himself up, his eyes reflected his condition. ". . . they shall lay hands on the sick, and they shall recover" (Mark 16:18). That's a promise God made to believers, not only to preachers, priests, prophets and evangelists, but to spirit-filled, born-again believers. So we prayed with all our hearts, believing that by his stripes we are healed.

After we prayed, Jerry said, "Rick, now go home and take your pill." Well, it turns out that the doctor had given him a prescription at the clinic for pain, and when he had left the trailer that morning, he had gone to the drug store to have it filled. While at the drug store, he felt in his spirit the Lord speaking to him saying, "Don't get that prescription filled. Go back to the trailer and get prayed for."

Looking at Jerry very surprised, he said, "What pain pills, what pills? I didn't get that prescription filled."

Jerry said, "I'm talking about the Gospel, Rick. Annie, write Rick out a prescription." So I wrote out: (1 Peter 2:24) ". . . by whose stripes ye were healed." But I wrote it this way: "By my stripes, Rick was healed."

Jerry said, "Rick, now repeat after me, 'By my stripes, Rick was healed . . . by my stripes, Rick was healed, amen.' Now Rick, when you go home, take those Gospels! Take one after dinner, one after supper, take two before you go to bed, and when you get up in the morning, take two more."

We went to the camp meeting that night and shared about how Rick had come to the trailer for prayer and how my husband had a word of knowledge for him.

"I'm expecting him to come tomorrow night," Jerry said, "to testify."

Our God is faithful. The next night, Rick walked through the door. We invited him to the front of the church to share with the people that God, praise God, had honored his word and healed his back.

God heals! Amen.

Footnote

If you're sick in body or spirit, you too can receive of God's healing power. Take a Gos-Pill. They're found in Isaiah 53:5 and 1 Peter 2:24. "O taste and see that the Lord is good . . . " Psalm 34:8. Then write us and share your healing. Our address is on the back pages of this book. Amen.

Impossible is not a word God uses! He can do all things if only we will be his hand extended.

Roll truck roll from Canadas extreme north, south to Alberta, and on to the supernatural beauty of the snow-capped Rocky Mountains. Just ahead is a . . .

B.C. Blessing

≈≈≈≋≋≈≈

Just below Dawson, a few miles south of the Alcan Highway, lies a little British Columbia town called Chetwynd. This was to be a night of nights because God was about to move in the altar service in a mighty way. The main service was over. We had sung hymns and lifted up Jesus; we had preached his powerful word; we had invited his Holy Spirit. Our Savior promised to send another Comforter, and he did that night. He came just as Jesus had promised. It was as if a blanket of heavenly love covered us. Faces shone with expectancy; many received.

The service had been dismissed, time had flown by, and many people had gone home. Only a few were left sitting around. When you give 100 percent of yourself, you're exhausted, so at the end of the service, I sat down in a pew. I was just sitting there when a native lady came over to me. She stood by the pew and said, "Sister Shaw, we sure had a good service tonight."

"Amen," I said. "Yes, we did. God was so real at the altar."

She was about to leave when I noticed that she had her hand tightly clenched. She was holding it close to her body.

I could see that her hand was swollen and discolored. I said, "Sister, did you get your hand caught in a car door or something?"

"No," she told me. "I had an operation nearly four months ago for carpel tunnel syndrome, and it just won't heal. My doctor made an appointment for me to see a specialist at two o'clock tomorrow."

I felt compassion rise up inside me. I reached up my hand, placed it over hers, and said, "As sisters in the Lord, and believers in the healing power of Jesus, let's agree together." I prayed, "Lord, would you please touch this sister's hand?" Astonished, she said, "Something is happening to me! My hand!" (A miracle is a supernatural, instantaneous move of God.) I hadn't expected him to move so fast. I mean, I was so tired. I just didn't expect God to move that quickly, but with God as my witness, the swelling was going down right in front of our eyes. A normal color was coming into her hand. Praise God!

She looked in amazement at the scar on her hand where they had operated. It had been healed. A minute ago, before we prayed, there was only bone and raw flesh. God touched her; right in front of our eyes the raw flesh knitted together. We watched it go together. Praise the Lord!

We could hardly believe our eyes, hallelujah. She began to move her hand back and forth excitedly, and said, "I haven't even been able to move my hand like this in four months." It was then that we became aware that the pastor of the church was looking on and excitedly praising God. We heard him say, "I haven't shouted like this in years!" He was bouncing all over the place. We found out later that he was a very reserved type, that he didn't do a lot of shouting. Well, he wasn't reserved that night, praise

God! Just to be in the presence of the Living God will excite anyone. Hallelujah!

I promise you, there is nothing impossible with God. It's not my word; it's my belief. Praise God, amen!

> Trust and obey,
> He'll make a way,
> To reach our
> Lost loved ones,
> We must trust
> And obey.

We tried the door of a small mountain town's variety store only to find it locked. We spotted a hand-written sign that read . . .

Gone Fishing

No question about it, the hardest people to witness to are those in your own family. It's been that way for me. But God will make a way, he'll open a window of opportunity if we pray through and wait on his timing.

I received an invitation from my brother, Bob, to go fishing. Of course, I said yes. Then added, "I'll bring my son along, too." I thought, "We'll only be gone for a couple of days." That was the plan. It would give me adequate opportunity to speak to them about their souls. (See Proverbs 11:30). At that time, both of them were unsaved.

We piled in a truck, with a boat trailer in tow, to drive 150 miles to a lake where Bob said he knew for sure we'd get fish—not just fish, but big fish! British Columbia is known to be a sportsman's paradise so we expected to have a wonderful time catching rainbow trout.

After they set the tent up for the night, they put the boat in the water intending to have everything ready for the morning. There were twenty-five miles of open water to cross, so they wanted to be sure that everything was working well. As darkness came upon them, they still couldn't get the big 55 hp motor to start.

Come morning, with the first light of day, they were working on the motor. I watched as they tried over and over to start the outboard, but the roar of the motor never sounded. They stopped long enough to eat breakfast, then continued trying. They didn't give up easily. Finally, they came to me and said, "Jerry, we can't seem to get that motor going! We'll try it with the small motor."

"Oh, Lord, no," I thought. A five-horsepower motor is hardly big enough to carry us over all those miles of open water. Twenty-five miles—that's a long way. Many things could go wrong. They assured me that since there was no wind, they could do it. I said, "Well, OK, if you're sure." They said, "We're sure." But as they packed the tent, I looked across the water and shuddered. I didn't feel so positive about it.

My motto is to pray, so I prayed, "Dear Lord, we didn't come here to drown. I pray that you would send a wind that will discourage them, Lord. I don't want to be a killjoy. I want to go along with whatever they come up with, but, Lord, they're not thinking sensibly. Send the wind—it will change their minds."

I had no sooner stopped praying and God moved. You could feel the wind come up. Within the next fifteen minutes, the water that had been so peaceful, now had white caps. They loaded the boat onto the trailer and sadly told me, "Jerry, we're sorry, we can't go. There's just too much wind—it would be too dangerous."

I said, "Well, I understand." I quickly turned my face away because I had no disappointed look to share with them. We drove back toward home to another lake that was much smaller. They set the boat in the water, we put our fishing rods in, reset the tent, then tried our luck. It wasn't long before most every cast was reaping a beautiful trout. It was magnificent! God was blessing us, amen.

As I sat there on the boat in the sunshine, I was not thinking about catching fish, but about the conversation of the night before. I had told my brother a little about God, as much as he was willing to listen to. Finally, I closed the conversation with this simple statement, "God will prove himself to you sometime during this trip. I'm 100% sure he will. Just wait."

HE'S GOD—EXPECT THE UNEXPECTED

I don't know what caused it, a blast of wind, or perhaps one of us moved too fast, but all of a sudden I saw my brother lunge into the air, do a somersault and land in the lake. He came up sputtering. These Rocky Mountain lakes are glacier fed, so we knew we had to move quickly. We grabbed him and hauled him into the boat. All he could say was, "I lost my rod. My wife bought that beautiful rod for me, it's a four hundred dollar rod." We looked into the lake, but couldn't see two or three feet down into the water, let alone to the bottom.

Soon he said, "I'm very cold. You'd better take me ashore."

"Well, sure, but let me make one cast for you and get your rod," I said.

"One cast?"

"Yes, one cast."

So I made one cast with a larger hook and more weight.

He looked at me and said, "If you get it, I'd have to believe there was a God, wouldn't I?"

"I hope so," I said.

After he finished talking, I began to pray, "Lord, in the name of Jesus, cause this line and hook to run across his fishing rod. Nothing is impossible for you, Lord. You know where his rod is. Lord God, prove yourself to my brother Bob. Amen."

Then very slowly, I began to wind it up. He said, "This is foolishness. You better take me to shore." Suddenly, I felt something on the line. I continued reeling. "I've got something!" They looked at me half laughing, as if I'd just told the best joke they'd ever heard. They were thinking I had just hooked a twig or something. The hook broke the surface and on it was a piece of nylon leader. I continued to wind it up, up, up, until finally his rod came up.

I'd asked God to prove himself to my brother, and he had, because the Holy Spirit had gone fishing with us!

FOOTNOTE

Shortly after that fishing trip, both my son and my brother Bob surrendered their lives to Jesus.

When it seems there's no direction to turn, look up! Your redemption draweth nigh; the answer is on the way!

Well, climb in the truck, close the door, fasten your seat belts, and let's push on due south across the Canada-United States border through Washington State, and on to Oregon—our destination—the City of Roses.

Good-bye Canada . . .

Hello Portland Oregon

~~~~~~~~

"Truck motor sounds great—it's purring like a kitten," I informed Annie as we drove toward the red light. Obligingly, it switched to green as if responding to our wishful thinking. I gunned the motor to speed us through the intersection. Our truck, like a Sherman tank, responded with a hearty roar, then instantly backfired like a supersonic airplane—boom! Oh Lord, now what? A wave of panic gripped us. Hello Portland, Oregon!

"What is it?", Annie asked. I told her we had just blown the motor. All I could think of was to hire a tow truck to pull us back to the church where we had just finished holding services. We began to weigh our options. After a week we were still nowhere. We couldn't afford a new motor; couldn't find a second-hand one; we couldn't this, and we couldn't that.

One morning I was scanning the newspaper for a motor when a car stopped beside our trailer and a man got out. He knocked, then, without invitation, opened the door and stepped in, and said, "I'm Norman Cox. I heard about your trouble. I've got it all worked out." He held in his hand a large notebook with two columns of figures, one for a gas motor, the other for a diesel.

"See for yourself. This is what it's going to cost," he said. He paused, glanced at me, and said, "Don't look so sad. Here's the first one thousand dollars." You could have knocked us down with a feather. "Oh, Lord, you haven't forgotten us," Annie sighed.

The only sure thing in Portland in the springtime is rain, rain, and more rain. Almost every day it's going to rain all day long. But even though it rained, our spirits remained high as we waited on God.

True to his word, Norman had given us a check in the sum of one thousand dollars. He even found a garage that would install the new motor. "But it will be a few days before they can get started," he told us. We laughed telling him, "Time we've got—we're long on time, you know, and short on money!" They towed our truck to the garage and put it in the compound to wait its turn.

We began everyday about the same: we'd pray, then study the Bible. (See 2 Timothy 2:15.) We had just opened our Bibles one day when someone knocked. A cheerful voice said, "Anyone up in there?"

"We're up—come on in." It was the assistant pastor of the church. "We were having Bible study. Would you like to join us?"

"Why, I'd love to," he replied. "Do you do this every day, I mean, study the Bible?"

"Why, yes, we do—every morning around ten o'clock."

"Could I bring my wife tomorrow?" The next day he brought his wife, and then it happened again. Another knock. It was one of the workers from the day-care center who had stopped by to invite Annie out for coffee and muffins. "I'd love to go after Bible study," Annie told her. "Would you like to join us?" And she did.

The next day, God's man, Norman, came by exactly at our Bible study time. He was quick to bring in his Bible from his vehicle. Before he left, he informed us that his wife would be with him the next morning, and she was. And so it went, with God adding daily whomever the spirit drew.

"What about the truck? How's it coming along?" folks would ask. One day, we drove by the garage to check on it. We found the gate locked; the doors rolled down. Nobody was there, so we phoned and phoned until finally, a sick-sounding voice told us, "Yes, we're closed. Everyone here has the old-fashioned flu. No choice but to wait it out." We did. Wait and wait and wait. Finally the garage was in operation again. At last came the phone call that we'd been waiting for. "Your truck's ready. Come and get it."

Together, Norman and I went to pick up the truck to test drive it. What a state it was in! We had the sickest new motor that you ever heard. Seems the staff had gone back to work weak and sick. They had used second-hand parts and rusty bolts to hold the truck together.

The Bible says we should "pray without ceasing" (1 Thessalonians 5:17).

HELP, LORD

"Lord, we are your servants. Don't let them get away with this injustice." Then we complained to the garage. The garage blamed the supplier, and the supplier said, "It's not our fault—it's your problem. We gave you perfect parts, a perfect motor. You installed them incorrectly." So they fought and fought, until finally, the supplier, a major dealer in the area, weakened and took our truck into their shop. Just about everything was wrong. They finally worked their way through it. Two motors later, they had us running well enough to go back on the road for Jesus. This time, as we neared the same intersection where we blew the motor, we knew that we'd make it through the red light. Once again, it obligingly turned green, and we pushed on the gas pedal to hasten us through the traffic signal.

See you later, Portland, Oregon!

The clang of a steel prison cell closing is anything but music to the ears of the prisoner. Paul and Silas prayed and sang praises unto God, suddenly there was a great earthquake and every prison cell door was opened and the captives were . . .

Set Free

~~~~~~~~~~

She stood there with her hands raised, praying. I thought in my heart I should go agree with her, so I went and placed my hand on her shoulder to pray. But somehow, I just couldn't. My mind went blank, and I lost all desire to agree. I didn't know what had happened, but I could not pray.

After the service, we joined the pastor and his wife for a cup of coffee. My mind, however, was back in church. I was still questioning, why couldn't I pray for that woman? I found myself saying to the pastor, "I don't know how you feel about me telling you this, but that woman has an unclean spirit." To my surprise, the pastor said, "Yes, I know." His wife said, "Yes, Sister Shaw, we knew. Why didn't you do something?"

I said, "I don't know. I really don't know."

The pastor's wife said, "God has revealed this to you. I am going to bring her to your trailer tomorrow so you can pray for her." I thought, "God, I really need your guidance now!"

The next day, true to her word, the two sisters arrived. They sat on the couch looking at me as Peggy spoke. "The pastor's wife told me what you said. Are you saying something unclean is in me?" I said, "Well, yes, Peggy, that's what I'm saying—that's what the Lord is telling me. There's something unclean." She began to sob. "I don't want this unclean thing!"

We laid hands on her, both agreeing in prayer for her deliverance. There are no words to properly describe God— he's magnificently awesome. Something happened in our trailer that day. Everything seemed brighter, a heaviness lifted. Just as darkness concedes daily to light, sin's evil blackness lost its battle. The unclean spirit left her.

We received a letter from her sometime later. The way she began really blessed our hearts. "Dear Brother and Sister Shaw, Thank God, I'm back home with Jesus!" She shared in her letter something I'd never even noticed. We had a little dog in our trailer, and she wrote that when we began to pray, and the evil thing left, the little dog began to snap and growl! We didn't even notice that because we were more interested in seeing our sister set free. This old chorus is her testimony.

> He set me free.
> Yes, he set me free.
> He broke the bonds of prison for me.
> I'm heaven bound, my Savior to see.
> Glory to God, he set me free!

I'll always recall Peggy's last words: "Thank God, I'm free!"

Often times as we share these victories we encounter people who are sceptics at best. They are full of doubt and unbelief. Some even say . . .

You're Kidding

There's no easy way to hide pain. It shows in the way a person stands or walks. You can hear it in the voice, and there's no mistaking it in the eyes—the eyes are the mirror of the soul.

Lillie came to the service in pain, desperately in need of a healing. At the time of the altar call, a word of knowledge was spoken, and it revealed exactly what she was suffering. But she said, "I didn't want to go forward. I'm not a real bold person. Besides, this healing might not be for me, it could be for someone else. So I just sat there. But inside me, I felt I should rise up and be healed in the name of Jesus. I felt I really should make the effort."

A Step of Faith

The Holy Spirit continued to draw her until she finally came forward. Jerry and I began to pray for her. Sometimes you just know that a person is healed. I felt that the Lord had touched her. I said, "Sister, I believe the Lord has blessed you."

Lillie replied, "Why yes, I believe he has too. I felt an intense heat on my back."

I said, "Well, why don't you try it out? Take a step of faith. Do something that you couldn't do before."

Her back had been giving her a lot of trouble for a long time. She'd seen many physicians, but nothing they had tried did much good. (See Luke 8:43.) I said, "Why don't you bend down and touch your toes?" She did, and with a look of amazement on her face, Lillie straightened up.

"Has the Lord touched your back, Sister?"

She said, "You know, I believe that he has."

"Well, why don't you try it again? Touch your toes." So she bent over, then straightened up again.

"How do you feel about it now? Did the Lord touch you? Twist around a little bit. Let's make good and sure that your back is OK." Lillie twisted her hips around a little, then looked at me.

"Well?"

"You know, I believe that I am healed."

"Sister, I believe that to show you have been healed, you need to take a step of faith. I believe that you ought to run down to that door and back again." She looked at me, startled because she had been talking to me in very low tones. She really didn't want anyone to hear us.

"You're kidding?"

"No, I don't believe I am, Sister."

"You really want me to run down to that door?"

"I really believe you should."

"You're kidding," Lillie said again, in a very serious voice.

God honors our baby steps of faith. She didn't quite make it down to the door, maybe halfway down, but the Spirit of the Lord honored her. God honored that step of faith—he loves us. When we make a step of faith, God honors and blesses. No kidding, amen.

Man has invented many powerful things, including guns and bombs, that can cause great destruction. But man in his wisdom is not even close to matching the almighty power of God's elements we call . . .

Storms

California is a beautiful state, especially from the Siskiyou Mountains south along the Pacific shoreline. Some of those mountains seem to almost reach heaven. Truly God has excelled here. But no state is more prone to disaster than sunny California. Floods take lives and cause serious damage year after year. But yet, the rain that causes these floods is a much needed blessing. The oranges, grapes, and everything that grows here, needs rain. Yes, California is dependent on the rain. However, all that rain causes mudslides in the Los Angeles area that claim lives and cause millions of dollars in damage.

Then there's the Santa Anna winds that blow hot and dry for weeks on end. All it takes is a spark to ignite uncontrollable fires that consume everything in their path.

And last, we must not fail to mention the earthquakes. They've had many, mostly small ones. But everyone who resides there lives with the constant threat that one day, someday, the big one is coming. Sort of sounds like the Lord, doesn't it? One day, in an hour we know not, he is coming. (See Revelation 3:3.) Praise the Lord!

A Big One

When we were ministering in California, I spoke to a number of people about the earthquakes. Many people who live there assured me that there was nothing to worry about. I said, "But you have a quake almost every day."

"Oh yes!" they said. "Sometimes even two or three, but they're small. Just little tremors; just rumblings—nothing to worry about. They haven't hurt us yet, have they?" they'd laugh.

But in my spirit I shivered, because after all, where there's smoke there's fire. Every day we were there, I felt a growing desire to leave the area. It intensified until about three days later when we left the Los Angeles area and headed for Phoenix, Arizona. We had just made it to Phoenix when radio, television, and newspapers were filled with news about the California quake disaster. Many lives were lost, buildings had crumbled, bridges collapsed. In all, countless damage; billions of dollars.

I recalled those folks laughing, and saying, "They haven't hurt us yet. They're just rumblings." But, oh how short is man's memory! Out, comes the construction equipment; up, go new buildings, and memories of the big quake resurface only in conversations of yesterday. How quickly we forget! It's like a woman bringing forth new life. The pain of the moment is soon lost in the victory cry of life from God's special creation.

We praised God for delivering us. That's not the only time that he has been faithful to us. Of course, it requires that we listen to his still, small voice and follow his instructions.

One time, we were making our way north from Baton Rouge, Louisiana, where we had spent time with our friend, an old saint in the Lord named Jimmy Davis. Jimmy was a precious man who had been singing gospel music most of his life. He'd given his heart to Jesus long before becoming the governor of the state.

As we traveled north through Louisiana into Arkansas, we felt a strange closeness in the air. It was not only dark and gloomy, there was something we could not quite put our fingers on. Every time we stopped for gas, people would mention the tornadoes that were touching down. The day wore on and by the time five o'clock had arrived, we were in a town called Fordyce, Arkansas.

I decided we'd gone far enough for the day and that I would give the pastor of one of the local churches a call to see if they were having a service. We often did this when we were en route from one series of meetings to another. Then we would continue on the next day. The pastor was a cheery person who quickly made us very welcome. He said, "Come on, come on!" But I found myself saying to him as I was about to hang up the phone, "Pastor, if we're not there in five or ten minutes, don't worry about it—it will simply mean that we've gone on to the next town." Then I hung up the phone.

When I got back to the truck, Sister Annie asked me if the pastor had made us welcome. I climbed into the truck and said, "Yes, he did, but we're going on to the next town." It's that still, small voice of the Spirit that we have got to listen to. I sensed an urgency to move on. Just keep moving.

The next town of any size was about thirty miles away. When we pulled into Rison, Arkansas, I phoned the pastor, and he also made us really welcome. As we pulled the trailer and truck in beside the church, along came the pastor to shake our hands. We talked with him, sharing about the powerful moving of the Holy Spirit we'd been seeing in our meetings. He asked us if we would consider taking the service that night. I said we'd be honored to.

"I don't know how many people will come," he said. "Did you hear about the tornado?"

"Yes, we've heard," we told him.

The service started around seven o'clock, and although the people came, you could see by the expression on their faces that they were concerned. We sang a few songs, then shared a victory or two. When the Lord sent us out into the ministry, his instructions were to "Go . . . and tell the good things the Lord hath done for thee . . . " (Mark 5:19).

Still, as we ministered that night, we found it was difficult to reach the people because of their anxiety. Finally, Sister Annie spoke up asking if they were concerned about the tornado. That was it—they were, and rightfully so. This was Arkansas, appropriately nicknamed Tornado Alley!

"Come to the altar," Sister Annie urged the people. "We'll join hands and hearts in prayer. We'll take authority in the name of Jesus over the storm. God will protect his children and your homes as well." Everyone stood and walked to the altar. Not long after that, the telephone began to ring in the church. The pastor scurried to answer it.

About that time, a young man who reminded us of the prophet, Elijah, felt impressed in his spirit to go outside the church, raise his hands toward heaven, and speak to God in prayer. He prayed that God would stop this dreaded tornado from coming our way. Meanwhile, inside the church we were united in prayer, imploring God to take this tornado and cause it to go out to sea. Shortly after that, we sensed that it had passed over. Praise the Lord, it had! It was then that the pastor shared with us about the telephone call. It seems the authorities had called to tell him, "Pastor, your church is right in the path of the tornado. Do what you must. Get your people to a safe place." But the spirit of the Lord had spoken to him as he hung up. "Don't do anything; just relax. I have everything under control."

God did have everything under control, praise God! Hallelujah! We prayed with many people around the altar and many received their healing. One woman, who was suffering from gout, was healed. The next day, in the restaurant where she was employed, she was able to share with the pastor, his wife, and us, just how wonderfully the Lord had healed her. There was no more pain—she could work as a healthy person again.

During our conversation, the pastor of the church informed us the tornado had touched down in the town where the Holy Spirit had prompted us to move on.

"It's caused considerable damage," he said. "They have fenced a section of the town because of debris."

Annie and I had never seen the devastation of a tornado firsthand, so we decided to drive back the thirty miles to see it with our own eyes. The tornado had come through that town destroying everything in its path. It had gone down one side of the street, turning trailers over, ripping roofs off, uprooting huge trees, breaking them off at the bottom as if they were twigs, while it left the other side of the street untouched. The area was pronounced a disaster area.

God is good. He had spoken to my spirit, "Keep on moving." We're so grateful to God that we did. What a blessing to hear the still, small voice of God. He has never changed. He still speaks to the listening heart. *It's one thing to pray, but the other part is to listen* to what God has to say. That still, small voice will direct our path all the way through this earthly walk and on glory. Amen.

Recently, we were in the Lone Star state of Texas, west of Dallas, when I felt an urgency in my spirit to head for Tennessee. Whenever I receive a holy nudge, I'm obedient to the Spirit. So I checked the road map and the shortest way was the middle route through Arkansas, which passed through many of the towns we'd ministered in before, including the town of Arkadelphia. As I looked at the map, contemplating distance, I felt in my spirit that God was saying, "Don't go that way. Go by Shreveport, Louisiana." After all these years of following the leading of the Holy Spirit, I know better than to argue, so I said to Sister Annie, "We're not going to go the way we originally planned. We're going by Shreveport, then up through Monroe."

As we traveled along through Louisiana, the radio kept informing us that they were expecting some heavy weather. There were warnings of potential tornadoes. The combination was just right; cold air from Canada pushing down and combining with warm, moist air from the Gulf of Mexico. As darkness came upon us that night, we were in a small village near the Louisiana-Arkansas border. We decided we'd stay there. It seemed like a good safe place. We'd no sooner hooked the trailer up for the night when the rain began. Within minutes it was raining cats and dogs! Buckets and buckets! Never had we seen such a rainstorm! It was as if the heavens had opened. We thought of Noah and the Ark. The light of the new day didn't change things. It continued to rain. The radio kept reporting that to the north of us, tornadoes were touching down. The announcer spoke of the devastation they had caused in exactly the town where we would have been if we had gone the original route. Once again God had spared our lives. Why? Because we're his servants! He's our God; He's our boss; He's an equal opportunity employer that looks after his employees. *One of his benefits is protection*

There were several lives lost in Arkadelphia. A major disaster, the media called it. To check it out, we went to the area but the military was there in full uniform with guns and road blocks to stop people from getting close and to prevent looting and keep people from hurting themselves with broken glass or live electric wires.

Again, we were able to say, "Thank you, Lord. You saved us again." The news media took many pictures of what had happened. Buildings that had stood the test of time were diminished to rubble.

I started thinking about it. God knows where these storms are coming from and where they are going. I was impressed the night before: "Don't go that way, go this way." So once again, God directed our path. I recalled reading about Brother Paul. The Lord told him not to enter a certain city. (See Acts 16:7-10.) Paul didn't go there because he would have been disobedient to God's Holy Spirit.

We never want to be disobedient to the Spirit, so we just keep moving, keep listening, keep our eyes looking up, our ears open; for soon, very soon, we will hear the sound of the trumpet, and with Jesus Christ, we will rise above these earthly storms, amen.

God knows what we have need of, and for that matter, what we *don't* require, as you're about to read in the next amazing blessing.

I Forgot My Watch

—⟨⟨⟨⟨⟨⟨⟩⟩⟩⟩⟩⟩—

Just a few miles west of Tucson, Arizona, up a narrow, winding road that cuts a path through a forest of saguaro cactus, far off the beaten track, is a village called Picture Rock. It's really just a wide spot in the road with a service station, a variety store, and a church where we were blessed to minister one Sunday.

In every service there's a variety of different needs represented. One woman, who came with a dire physical need, informed the pastor's wife that she couldn't stay until the end of the service because she had a husband at home to fix lunch for. He had to be at work at a certain hour and that meant she would have to leave the service early.

"That's too bad—we're having Sunday dinner here at the church," the pastor's wife informed her. "We'd love to have you stay."

"Sorry," she said with a note of regret in her voice. "I'll have to miss it. Duty calls." Sitting there in the service, knowing time was going by quickly, she glanced at her arm and realized that she had left her watch at home. Since there was no clock on the wall, she looked at the arms around her, hoping to spot someone's watch, but as she said later, everybody must have forgotten their watches as well. God works in mysterious ways to perform his wonders. God had something for her that she would have missed if she left early. This was her day for a miracle!

At the end of the service, we called people forward for prayer. Those that had needs came forward with them. She came to the altar to receive her healing, no longer caring about time, knowing that she had a need that only God could meet. So we prayed for her. Her back had been bothering her for many years. We touched her. The Bible says that if you lay hands on the sick and pray the prayer of faith, they will recover. *Nothing is impossible with God.* No matter how old the injury is, no matter how long the heavy load of sickness has been carried, time means nothing to God. *His healing power is for now.* So we touched her. We prayed, not with our heads, hoping, but as believers, with our hearts positive of our God. After prayer, we asked her to bend over and touch the floor, then to twist her waist around. She did, and all of her pain was gone.

God doesn't miss anything. The pastor's wife saw that it was getting late. She hurried to the kitchen to prepare two plate lunches.

"Here, Sister, I think you better hurry home and feed your husband." God knows everything. He knew her obligations. The Lord, praise God, meets all our need. (See Phillipians 4:19.) We thank God that she received a wonderful miracle healing from God. She is now a walking testimony of God's love, amen. She'll never forget that she's been healed by God.

She came back in the evening to share what God had done, and when she stood to testify it went like this: "This morning when I came to church, I had forgotten my watch, and I'm glad I did. . . ."

Through life as we travel we will encounter many testings. Often we will trudge through long dry deserts. But do not lose heart weary pilgrim. Ahead there is a cool running river where a refreshing drink is waiting for you. Be not concerned about the mountain that looms in the distance; this is not the first one you've climbed. Child of God, there will always be . . .

Another Mountain

Some days are unforgettable. They are destined to remain a lifetime memory. Leaving Las Cruces, New Mexico, we picked up Highway 70 East, en route to our next meeting in northern Texas. "It's a dry, thirsty land," I thought as the wind whipped up little dust twisters.

"They sure need rain, Annie," I said.

"Yes," she replied. "They sure do. When was it we saw rain last?"

"Not since California," I told her, "That's nearly three months ago."

"Would you believe it? I've missed the rains and snow," she smiled.

The map showed the mountain range, but I didn't see the elevation, so I figured it wasn't much. Bad mistake. We began to climb the Ruidosa Mountain—up, up we climbed. It was a heavy pull that made our old Chevy prove itself. Our truck gave it's all—it was pedal to the metal all the way to the summit. Almost instantly, along the plateau, we picked up speed to about fifty miles per hour

when, without any warning, we started down the east slope
of the mountain. There were no signs that read "steep hill"
or "steep grade." Nothing whatsoever. Within seconds,
we were running at over seventy miles per hour and gain-
ing speed! Our truck motor was screaming, wide open.

"Oh Lord," we cried. We tried repeatedly to slow down,
but we couldn't do anymore than push the brakes. We couldn't
turn the key off. If we did, we'd lose all control as the steering wheel locked. Oh no, it was even worse ahead: we could
see a long curve in the road and a sign that said Slow Down
and Live.

"Annie," I yelled, "If there ever was a time to pray, it's
now!" So Annie prayed while I kept pumping on the brakes
and steering the truck. In my heart of hearts, I was thinking, is this where it's all going to end? Are we going to be
with the Lord Jesus today? The motor roared at full throttle
as we entered the curve. We were still going close to seventy miles per hour when I spotted another sign that indicated forty miles per hour as a safe speed. Oh, God!

Miracle of miracles! Somehow we made it, and the road
straightened out, although the hill continued. A little mountain town loomed up ahead with an intersection and a red
traffic light. Both Annie and I were praying because we knew
that there was no way we could stop. Our motor was still
revved up to the maximum. So with our horn blowing, we
crossed the intersection still doing nearly fifty miles an hour.

On the way out of the small town, the road started up a
long, straight hill. It was here that we threw our gear shift
into neutral and finally coasted to a complete stop. Whew!
What in the world caused this? I climbed out and raised
the hood as bewildered as I had ever been in my life. I
searched and re-searched, tapped this and pushed that, then

looked some more but found nothing. Then I pulled off the carburetor cover and spotted a spark plug wire lodged in the linkage of the gas pedal. Seems that going up the mountain, the linkage had opened just wide enough to allow the wire to fall in and to keep the motor running at full speed. Ah, yes! There is a real devil loose!

A few miles ahead, along the road lay north Texas with it's easy-rolling prairie land. We gave God the honor, the glory, and the praise, for there was no question that he had spared our lives. God smiled on our Sunday services in Texas. Jesus had said he would send another Comforter, and he did. He sent the Holy Spirit to our meetings. At the service that night, the weather changed. First it rained—Texas-style. Big-time rain! Then it turned to sleet and hail, blown along by a powerful wind. It was as if God said, "So you miss the rain, do you?" Then came the snow.

The next morning, we woke up to a sunny, snowy, cold, icy, Texas day, praise the Lord! 1 Thessalonians 5:18 says, "In everything give thanks: for this is the will of God in Christ Jesus concerning you." Two days later we headed for southeast Texas, knowing full well that we'd have to go all the way to the Appalachians before we'd face another mountain.

Our God can do everything: heal broken hearts and lives; restore hopeless marriages; heal every sickness and affliction; open blind eyes; even make . . .

The Dumb Speak

We were en route to Texas, traveling through Louisiana, just north of New Orleans when darkness caught us in a little bayou town. What lay ahead was to be a most unforgettable experience. We had made contact with a pastor, and he welcomed us. We told him we would be attending church the following day, Sunday. He invited us to minister in song. After the morning service, we decided to continue west toward Texas, so we said good-bye and went to the trailer.

Annie was inside cooking lunch when a well-dressed man with a Bible tucked under his arm came along. He said that he had enjoyed the service, then asked if we'd like to go out to a restaurant for dinner. I said, "Thank you for inviting us, but my wife is already fixing us something to eat. We are going to get back on the road after lunch. We'd like to arrive at our destination before dark."

The man said OK. Then, pointing at one of our tires he said, "See that you get that fixed before you go too far." I looked where he was pointing, and, sure enough, the tire looked like it was going flat. When I looked under the trailer, I found it was more than just a low tire. One of the shackles on the trailer was about to break loose. The metal had torn away from the frame. It was weakened to the breaking point and couldn't have lasted more than a few more miles at best.

I turned to thank our friend for making us aware we had a problem, but he had disappeared. "Take your time making lunch," I told Annie, "We can't move a wheel until we have this fixed. In fact, forget about going anywhere today. We can't leave here until we get this welded back into place."

Evening came and I told the pastor that we would be there overnight.

"We have trouble with the trailer," I explained, then added that I wanted to say thanks to the man who had pointed it out.

As I was talking to the pastor and the church board, who came walking by but the brother who had pointed out our problem. I said, "Here comes the man now who told us about the problem with the trailer." The pastor and the men that were with him gave me a strange look.

"Are you sure that's the man?" they questioned.

"Yes indeed, that's the man." They looked at each other, then back at me, and said, "He can't talk. All he can do is utter sounds. He can't form words; he never has."

We serve a never-changing God! Opening the eyes of the blind or causing the dumb to speak are but a few of his miracles. There was no question that this was the hand of God—his hand of protection. He's the same yesterday, today, and forever! Praise the Lord!

The next morning around eight o'clock, Annie looked out the window and there was a welding truck pulling up.

He had come to work on our trailer. He set about doing the necessary repairs to get us back on the road for Jesus. After he had shut off his welding machine and was loading his equipment, I went to him and said, "How much do we owe you?" He quickly took out a notebook and began to work out a price. Then he wrote out a bill and reached out his hand to pass it to me. That's when someone from the church came out and snapped it out of his hand, and said, "We'll take care of that."

So you see, God is still moving and taking good care of his children. Yes, the dumb still speak. And yes, yes, yes "God shall supply all of your need according to his riches and glory by Christ Jesus" (Philippians 4:19). Revelation 12:7 mentions a war in heaven caused by Satan. It continues to tell us that Michael and his angels are victorious, praise the Lord. But it does not end there—in Revelation 12:12, God's Word says, ". . . Woe to the inhabiters of the earth . . . for the devil is come down unto you having great wrath . . . " Hey! There's a real devil loose on planet earth! We are not well kept secrets.

God knows us inside out. After all, he's our creator. He speaks to the little child in us he says, "Come." It's as simple as A-B-C. All you need to do is pray earnestly with a sincere heart. I'll never forget praying, then telling our Lord that I'm a simple man. Would He please, give me a simple . . .

Yes or No

=~~~~~~=

In the back pages of this book, we make mention of our tapes. Of course they're gospel music, mostly songs that the Lord has given us over the years. But back before I was saved, I had a country band. We'd play the bars and dance halls, places like that. I wrote secular songs back then. After my salvation (after I gave my heart to Jesus), I began to wonder about those songs. God had called us, now we were in the ministry, traveling the road for Jesus. Times were thick and thin; sometimes a feast, sometimes a famine. So I asked the Lord, "Lord, you know there's been considerable interest from the people in Nashville in our secular music. What if I release these songs and let Nashville record them? I'll use the money to help support ministries, missions, and do whatever the Spirit bids."

HE'S A PERSONAL SAVIOR

I continued praying, adding, "Lord, it seems like such a good idea to me. What should I do?" I asked the Lord for an answer but didn't get one. But one thing I know is, the squeaky wheel always gets the grease, so I prayed again. "Lord, I'm a simple man, please give me a simple yes or no."

That night, after we'd gone to bed and my dear wife was sound asleep beside me, I lay there praying about the music. "Dear Lord, what about that music? All I asked you for was a simple yes or no."

THE ANSWER IS ON THE WAY

Suddenly, almost like someone had switched on a video, in vivid, living color, this vision came to me: I saw a big hill. My eyes traveled up to the top where there was a large cross. As I was watching the cross, it seemed to rise out of the ground and come down the hill, end over end over end, right at me. I sat straight up in bed. I said, "Oh, no!" Immediately, I knew in my spirit that this vision was from God. He had just spoken to me, through me. I asked him for a yes or a no. I realized that God had answered me with a definite no.

His Word clearly states in Philippians 4:19, that ". . . my God shall supply all your need . . . " He's a personal Savior. He knows what's best for his children. Pray from your heart, with all your heart. He wants to hear from you. Go ahead, ask him yourself about your needs. He does not deal in ifs, or buts, or maybes. He won't leave you guessing. Just ask him for a simple yes or no.

God is not limited in his methods of healing, as you'll read in . . .

Punched and Pinched

—⟳⟳⟳—

M y name is Alice. I've never been slain in the spirit before. I guarded against it because, as you can see for yourself, I'm a large woman. I thought if someone tried to catch me, maybe they couldn't and perhaps I'd get hurt. I had all kinds of reasons why I couldn't, or shouldn't, be slain in the spirit." Alice had many health problems, including rheumatoid arthritis, a tumor in her sinuses, and another in her stomach that she said was so tender that when she tried to wash her dishes, she would have to guard against touching her sink because it caused her pain. There was no question that she needed a healing!

As we began to pray for Alice, Jerry felt led of God for me to lay my hand on her stomach area. Then he called six members of the church to come lay their hands on mine, one hand on top of the other. Last of all, the pastor put his hand on the top of ours. Then my husband tapped the pastor's hand as an act of faith and Alice went down! She didn't have time to stop and think of anything such as her size, or if someone would catch her. She was instantly in the spirit on the floor, praise God. She had yielded to God. Now healing could flow through her. She was again a little child on her father's knee. Later, when she got to her feet, her testimony was that she was healed.

Alice came to the trailer the next day and said, "I felt like somebody punched me in the stomach. Brother Shaw, I thought. You know, that tumor is gone from my nose. He put his forefinger along the outside of my nose, and it felt like he pinched my nose.

"I thought Brother Shaw had punched me and pinched me!" she said. But now I realize that it was not Brother Shaw at all, it was Jesus Christ. He made me every whit whole, praise his name!"

FOOTNOTE

As adults, our subconscious mind can hinder us from receiving from God. Little children have no problem accepting without question. Sometimes, as he did with Alice, God will bypass our subconscious mind to allow his healing stream to flow, but most of the time, he waits for us to surrender ourselves to him. Give up, and be healed in the name of Jesus!

God the Father wants us, his children, to have the very best gifts. Many times, he waits for us to rise up and come to the altar like . . .

Mr. Ed

━━━〰〰〰━━━

Due to insufficient demand, coupled with low world copper prices, we regret to inform you that mining operations will be suspended indefinitely" . . . and, so an era ended. Today, only rusty equipment and decaying buildings, covered by a heavy coating of copper dust, testify to past prosperity.

It was Valentine's Day and we were scheduled to minister an "I Love Jesus" service. It was here that we met Mr. Ed. Ed was on the church board and as active as his health would allow him to be. He had suffered a long time. He had Barr's Syndrome (a chronic condition), coupled with hepatitis that left him tired all the time. He also had growths on his body that caused him extreme concern. The one on his stomach had begun to change color and size (a sign of cancer). There was another one on his leg, and yet one more on his lip that faced him every time he shaved.

"My doctors haven't given me a bright future," he said.

"There's no real cure, only Band-Aids," they had informed him. "But you never know, they could come up with a cure tomorrow."

"They tried to console me to keep a thread of hope connected, but inside I knew from the way I felt, I wouldn't be alive a long time." There was no question that Ed needed a miracle.

The Word of God says in James 5:14-15, "... the prayer of faith shall save the sick, and the Lord shall raise him up . . . " Here's a great recipe: blend together three units of faith in Jesus, add to it three units of belief in the Holy Spirit, mix in a tri-fold measure of love—there's nothing greater—then apply with hands of expectation, and watch God move, amen.

Mr. Ed was prayed for at the altar that night. God, who knew Mr. Ed inside and out, decided that this was his night for a major overhaul. Ed later told us about the intense heat that flowed through his body, but even he didn't know the full extent of God's miracle healing power at that time. However, in the morning, he felt stronger than he had for several years. Then as he shaved, he noticed the growth on his lip was gone. Yes, completely gone! And the growths on his stomach and leg had disappeared, removed by the scalpel of the Holy Spirit. No scars; healed; a 100% miracle.

Ed later visited his doctors and was declared healed of Barr's Syndrome, praise the Lord! He stood to testify and it was recorded on tape. First, he gave all glory to God for his healing, then he continued. "As you know, I'm on the church board. I was against having the Shaws come to minister at our church because I felt our church had had enough evangelists for a while. I thought we couldn't afford them. I knew all they asked was a love offering, but regardless, I voted them down. I'm so thankful to God that my vote was overruled. I'm totally healed, all praise and glory to God! Thank you, Jesus."

Before we left town, someone said the mine might re-open if the price of copper went higher. It was a statement—that amounted to wishful thinking. I thought to myself, "Sounds like a definite maybe to me."

Enjoy your Valentine gift, Mr. Ed.

A child's love is pure: without question, without doubt. That's why our Lord said to allow the little children to come unto him, as you'll read in . . .

Mississippi Monday

—=≈≈≈≈≈≈—

L ike diamonds sparkling in the sunshine, little towns
and hamlets dot both sides of the muddy Mississippi as
it snakes its way south to the Gulf of Mexico. Our friend,
Larry, a tall, soft-spoken man, pastored a church in the area.
He had invited us to come minister with him. We arrived
on Friday. The first thing we noticed was a For Sale sign on
his property. I commented on it, and he informed me that,
yes indeed, his property was for sale. He really needed to
sell it because he wanted to move closer to town. He'd found
another house, put a deposit on it, but had less than a week
to finalize the transaction or lose the house.

"Would you pray about it, Jerry? I mean, both you and
Annie. Would you pray?" We said, "Sure, Larry, let's pray
right now."

We've learned in the past that when requested to pray,
don't procrastinate. It's best to do it immediately because
some of that back-burner praying gets pushed off the stove
altogether. We'd never before prayed for a property to sell,
but why not? God's Holy Spirit can do anything, including

selling real estate, amen. So we prayed, "Lord, Larry is your servant. He needs to sell this house and land. Surely there's someone you can direct this way?"

It was on a Friday, close to supper time, that we prayed. The Lord didn't send anyone in until the next morning around ten o'clock. They just loved everything they saw—the land, the little barn out back, the color of the house, the way the house was laid out inside, the paint, everything. Talk about love at first sight!

"We'll go to the bank on Monday morning and arrange the money. Oh, and here's a binder to seal our offer," they said, as they wrote out a sizable check. True to their word, on Monday morning they went to the bank and everything was approved. The sale went through without a problem. The Holy Spirit is a super real-estate salesman!

But wait, I skipped Sunday.

That Sunday is now recorded in the pages of "His Story." Monday morning came to the Mississippi Delta area with a sunny, warm promise of a magnificent day to follow. We'd seen God's hand at work around the altar the night before. There had been salvations, baptisms, and many healings. We'd all gone home high on "new wine," but today was a "Mississippi Monday," and the ladies of the church were meeting in the sanctuary. I could hear them, even though the doors were closed. I was in the entrance of the church packing up our musical tapes when a little girl, about five years old, came walking up to me. She said, "Y'all prayed for my friend last night. She was healed." I had quite a problem understanding her. She had a sweet little southern accent. She said, "Would y'all pray for me?"

"I'd be happy to pray for you, honey," I said. "What do you want me to pray for?" She then told me that she had a problem with her right ear. I said, "Well, OK, we'll pray about it right now."

"OK, but please don't pray loud. I don't want everyone in there to hear," she said, pointing toward the sanctuary.

"All right, we won't pray loudly. Let's kneel down right here," I said, and we did. I held her little hands in mine and prayed, "Oh, dear Lord, you said yourself to allow the little children to come unto you, and to forbid them not, for such is the kingdom of God. Your words continue, dear Lord, that we all, regardless of age, must enter the kingdom of God as a little child." (See Mark 10:14.)

There's never any doubt whatsoever in little children. She had come asking God to heal her, and God never turns little children away. She was instantly healed! All glory to God!

The little girl went back into the sanctuary to be with her mother while I finished packing up our tapes. A few minutes later, her mother came by to thank me for praying for her daughter. She was totally healed! We all rejoiced in what God had done. It sure was a magnificent Mississippi Monday!

So many searching hearts are needing the truth to set them free; needing more than ifs, buts, and maybes. Wanting straight answers to find the way. Lord, we give you the honor, the glory and the . . .

Praise

The bright morning sunshine burned its path through the foggy mist that seemed to rise up to meet it in defiance only to disintegrate into a wisp as it became part of the haziness of the Smoky Mountains.

Over the phone, a woman gave me directions to her home. As she spoke, I jotted them down. "Take highway 111 south," she said. "Toward Spencer. You'll see a sign: McMinville. Go about five miles to a flashing light; turn left, then go a mile and a quarter to the stop sign, turn right. Be sure to count the farmhouses because we're the seventh house on the right side. You'll see the sign, Dogs for Sale; you can't miss it."

We followed her directions. Did she say you can't miss it? It was only after we'd given up altogether, turned the car around and headed home that we spotted the sign, Dogs for Sale. Her house sat well off the main road; it was built on a hill. We stopped the car in the yard, got out and were welcomed by barking dogs of all sizes, colors, and breeds.

We thought we were looking for a peek-a-poo pup. After meeting Wilma, the owner, she took us to a mother peek-a-poo with five beautiful puppies. They were cuddly-cute and would have made any home a little brighter, but for some reason we couldn't make up our mind. Which one shall we take? Which one? Which one?

We were given a grand tour of the kennels. She had beautiful dogs, this Wilma. Rare dogs, expensive dogs. All pure-bred dogs "with papers," she said. In one cage, she had a mother Pomeranian with her three little puppies, two males and one female. We paused because we were instantly smitten. We asked her how much and she told us. We looked at each other, and although we hadn't said a word, we read each other's eyes. After all these years of marriage, we both knew only too well the "too much" look. We continued on walking back toward the car, intending to leave, when the conversation turned to who we are, where we're from, and what we were doing in this area. We recognized this as an opportunity to tell this woman something about Jesus. We believe in walking through every door that the Holy Spirit opens, so we began to share.

An SOS

We were sitting in the truck and Wilma was standing by the window on Annie's side. It was easy to see that she was troubled in her spirit, but she listened as we shared Jesus with her. Finally she said, "Well, seeing as you people do what you do, would you please answer a few questions for me?" When somebody says that, you just never know where the questions are coming from or what they'll be, so it was time for a quick prayer to the Lord for help—an SOS to God—and that's what I did.

Then I said, "Surely, if we can." Wilma was like a loaded gun. Pointed, with hammer cocked, she fired her round of questions. "How come," she said, in a trembling voice, "How come there's so much homosexuality all of a sudden? Like on the TV and radio? How come everyone thinks it's all right. It never used to be, did it?"

I thought, "What a question. Bang on. Help, Lord."

We explained to her that we are living in the last days, and, as the word of God says, evil will increase. "People will call good, evil and evil, good. In a word, Wilma, it's prophecy happening, just as our Savior said it would. Wilma, look. It's in your Bible." She had already told us that she had a Bible. "Everything we're telling you, Wilma, can be backed up in God's word.

"The reason these things bother you so much is because you need peace yourself. Wilma, you need Jesus. You need to accept him into your heart and into your life, then these things will not bother you quite to the extent that they do now."

We just knew in our hearts that God was calling Wilma to make a commitment. So right there in the yard with her standing beside the window of the truck, Sister Annie took Wilma's hand in hers while I held onto Annie's hand, and together we prayed. Tears flowed as she invited Jesus to come into her heart. What a transformation!

What a presence of the Holy Spirit as she gave her heart to Jesus! And oh, the peace that flooded her as she turned her life over to him! Peace, peace, wonderful peace, coming down from the Father above. You could see the difference after Wilma gave her heart to Jesus. She changed so dramatically. She was now a bubbly little girl filled with peace beyond measure and joy unspeakable! She invited us into her home where she told us, "I can't really afford to just give you this pure bred Pomeranian puppy, but let me do this. I'll give her to you at a price that you can afford."

We named our little puppy blessing, "Praise," and like everything else we had, she became a valuable tool for Jesus. Sometimes opportunities to minister on a one-to-one basis would open up after people would ask the dog's name. Often they'd say, "How come you named your dog Praise?"

"So glad you asked that question . . . ."

Sometimes our road of life is as dry and dusty as a desert. But if we keep on keeping on soon we will see the palm trees surrounding . . .

The Oasis

~~~~~~~~~~

Among the many churches we've ministered in over the years, several have risen up as "refreshment stations" for us. We considered them spiritual oases. But there's one church that stands head and shoulders above all the others. It's in Tennessee.

We would arrive there like thirsty camels, and we were always made welcome. Pastor Pop Lowery and his jewel of a wife, Abby, really knew how to roll out the red carpet. Pastor Pop was continuously bringing in evangelists. He loved the Word and couldn't get enough of God! He'd start every day on his knees at the church, crying out for souls to be saved. Then he'd preach a live radio program from 7:30 until 8:00 A.M. What a man! Throughout the day, he did landscaping work. He'd always be the first back in church to pray again before the service in the evening. Clearly, Pastor Pop was on fire for God! I thought, "Now there's a man who loves God with all his heart" (See Matthew: 22:37).

We had just arrived when Pastor Pop in his excited voice told us, "We've got an evangelist tonight. You're going to enjoy this man. He's real different, his name is Tommy Hawk. He's from Ohio. What a ministry! Service starts about seven. Would you minister in song for us?" We said, "Yes, thank you for asking. We'll be happy to." But something came up, and Jerry was unable to attend the service that night, so I went by myself.

The service was definitely different from most. The atmosphere was charged with the Holy Spirit; people were excited. They were expecting something to happen. I sat by the pastor's wife, watching in amazement as people came forward for prayer and fell in the Spirit, some laughing, others crying. The evangelist, Tommy Hawk, walked into the congregation, right up to me and said, "Wouldn't you like God to touch you like that?" Well, I was more than a little bit skeptical. In fact, I was thinking, this can't be of God. So I told him, "No, I'll just sit here and enjoy the service."

Don't get me wrong. When Jerry and I pray with people, many times they fall in the Spirit and are healed, but I had never seen anything quite like this.

After the service, back in my trailer, I decided to check it out through God's Word. So with Bible and concordance I prayed, "Lord, is this ministry on the level?" I didn't want any part of it if it wasn't, and yet I didn't want to miss out on any great move of God either. So I prayed, "Lord, please show me." I searched for several hours but couldn't find anywhere that it would seem out of order.

The next morning I went to the Bible study more open-minded, determined to receive as much as I could. The evangelist spoke about the service the night before. He said that some folks were bound in self-righteousness and religious bondage. "One woman," he continued, "whom I had invited to the alter to receive a touch from God was frightened, and said, 'I'll just sit and enjoy the service right here.'"

"Why, you little twirp," I thought. "That's me you're talking about. How dare you!" So I closed my Bible and just sat there waiting for the service to end. But as he closed, he invited the ladies to come for prayer. All of them, except me, stood up and went to the altar. Now what Lord? I didn't want to cause dissension. The pastor and his wife are good friends. "Lord, what should I do?" I wanted Jerry to come to the service that night to see what his opinion would be, so I thought I better go up front with the rest of the ladies. I could hear the ladies being prayed for and falling in the Spirit. The next thing I knew I was falling in the Spirit, too! I was worshipping and experiencing a touch of God beyond anything I had ever known before. Later, I went to the evangelist and told him my resentment of him because of what he had said. He very gently told me that it wasn't me he was talking about.

That night at the service, Jerry and I took it all in. At altar time, I went forward; it was as if a magnet were drawing me. Jerry had this to say after we got home: "Annie, he didn't even touch you, and you were slain in the Spirit!" It didn't end there. It continued every service for the next several days, the same story over and over. Jerry said he couldn't believe it. He couldn't even count the many times I was hit by the power of God.

The time came for us to move on. We could attend just one last meeting. At the end of the service, the evangelist called both of us forward. We came, holding hands. He said, "This kind of thing is going to happen in your services." Jerry asked, "When, Brother?"

"The very next service," he said.

The next day we moved on to the mountain country of Tennessee and joined some dear friends that had just come down from Canada to visit us. To be with friends is always an oasis for us, but this was even a greater blessing because our Dutch-Canadian friends, Bram and Koss, were to meet our American-German friends, Vern and Barb.

On Sunday morning we all went to church together. The pastor asked us to minister the evening service. We didn't sing a lot, only a few songs. We didn't preach a lot either, but we did invite God's Holy Spirit to come, and he came with a powerful, fresh anointing to the altar service. We asked our friend, Bram, to come and stand behind folks in case they fell in the Spirit when the power of God touched them. Brother Bram came and almost instantly a cloud of holiness shrouded the altar. Everyone who came forward that night, the pastor included, was slain in the Spirit.

Our friend Bram later told us that his arms and back were sore from catching so many.

WHAT GOOD DOES IT DO?

But there's always someone with a question, and Bram's wife had one. She said, "All that falling in the Spirit. What good does it do?" It caused us to think, she's right, what good does it do? So we prayed, "Lord, Lord, what good does it do?"

The answer came a week later, in a meeting just south of Nashville, Tennessee. All heaven had broken loose. A tingle of excitement ran up and down every spine in the building, as the electrifying Holy Spirit arrived. A young woman suffering with a chronic back problem that her mother said she'd had since she was a child, came forward.

Jerry reached out his hand to touch her and she fell, slain in the Spirit. As she lay there touched by the Holy Spirit, we could see that her right leg was much shorter than her left one. Jerry felt led to pray for her shorter leg, but before he did, he invited everyone to come forward to witness what the Lord was about to do. Then he knelt down and laid hands on her foot, asking God to line her leg up even with the other one. (See Mark 16:17.)

He prayed with all his heart but nothing happened. So after a while, he stood and walked several feet away. He later told me that God began dealing with him, telling him to go back and pray for the longer leg. But Jerry said, "Lord, I don't have the heart to pray for anything right now, especially legs."

However, the Holy Spirit doesn't give up. God is no quitter. He kept nudging Jerry until he said, "All right, Lord." He again placed his hand on the young lady's foot and prayed. Needless to say, every eye in the building was watching the scene. All of a sudden, the longer leg snapped back even with the other and her back was totally healed. (See Mark 16:20.) Then came the still, small voice that said, "That's what good it does. That's what good it does."

Thanks to Jesus the chains of our past no longer hold us captive. Like Paul and Silas we can say . . .

I'm Free

〜〜〜〜〜

Words could never paint a picture to describe the beauty of the valley our eyes feasted upon. Farms dotted the rolling hills, orchards of fruit trees, some with lingering blossoms, gave off a sweet fragrance as if to advertise the harvest to come. Like frosting on a perfect cake, a clean river flowed onward to it's salty destination.

Revival had come to this valley many years before. Folks had taken a strong stand for God and, as Matthew 18:20 says, "For where two or more are gathered in my name, there am I in the midst of them." God had heard their prayers and held back the forces of evil that had attempted to pollute this near-heavenly paradise. But that generation graduated to glory, and after their departure, the old issues resurrected. This time sin prevailed. Like the river in a time of flooding, evil flowed into many lives. Alcohol, gambling, illicit sex, and drugs. Only memories remained of when morals were higher. But a remnant of Christians still prayed, believing that God would breathe new life into this valley of dry bones.

Like a beacon above it all, standing clean and white, was a little country church. The pastor opened the first service of the revival voicing his high expectations.

"Enter in and receive," he encouraged as he introduced us.

Some folks come to a full-gospel service to speculate as to what is going on while others come to participate. Some come to analyze and criticize, while others come to receive and achieve. The Holy Spirit never goes one step beyond our willingness, amen.

At altar time, the line between belief and doubt widens. Some come to Jesus at the altar, while others walk through the church doors and leave. It's always a step of faith to come to the altar. That night, many came making first-time commitments to Jesus. He met their needs of salvation, baptism, and healing. One young man needed deliverance. Although only seventeen, Bruce had been involved with major drugs and alcohol, and he'd been in trouble with the law. He lived with his grandparents who were always frightened of what he might do next. Recently, he had tried to burn down their house, but all that had changed a week or so before when Bruce invited Jesus to come into his heart to be the Lord of his life. Now he stood at the altar in need of deliverance. Somehow he reminded us of the man called Legion, mentioned in Luke 8, because he had so many devils. Bruce had also come to Jesus out of the tombstones of his life crying out to be free.

Sister Annie laid her hands on Bruce and prayed for his deliverance. She rebuked Satan while we all agreed in prayer. She prayed out loud, "The Lord, rebuke thee, Satan!" Bruce fell to the floor. Almost instantly, the demons manifested themselves. His body twisted and jerked. He was in torment. A growling, angry, violent noise came out of him that frightened many. There is nothing pretty about an angry devil—many folks ran for the door! We continued in Jesus' name to rebuke Satan, and as suddenly as it started, it stopped. He seemed peaceful. We praised God for his deliverance.

Later, we asked Bruce how it felt to be free. He told us, "There's more." He was right. The next night it happened again. A repeat performance from Satan and the forces of evil. They fought hard to hold onto their prize, but *God always prevails*. Once again, Bruce received deliverance. We said to him before he left to go home, "You're free, Bruce. You're delivered."

"No," he responded, "I'm not. Not yet. There's more." And it continued the next night. Again, Annie laid hands on him and prayed. We all agreed, and again he went down in a heap on the floor. Again, we saw the manifestations of demons from hell.

"He has a lying spirit," came a word of knowledge. The pastor's son held Bruce's head tightly in his hands and asked him point blank, "Do you have a lying spirit?" A strange voice came from Bruce's mouth: "Nooooo!" it said. As he lay there, we again took authority in Jesus' name. The scripture says that where two or more agree, they can rebuke a lying evil spirit. We ordered the lying spirit to leave him. Oh! There's power in the name of Jesus. Satan is no contender for God. The peace that passes all understanding flowed as Bruce became still and peaceful. While we watched, his chin began to quiver at a speed impossible for a human. Then his mouth opened and a beautiful, glorious, heavenly language came forth. God had baptized him in the Holy Spirit. We didn't have to ask him if he was free; now he was praising God and telling everybody, "I am free!"

He whom the Son sets free is free indeed! The last words we heard Bruce say as he left the church that night were, "Thank God, I'm free!"

FOOTNOTE

We recently heard that Bruce is studying to become a minister of the gospel. Amen.
Now she resides on the resurrection side of the cross.
You will be blessed when you meet sister . . .

Mildred

———≈≈≈≈≈———

Mildred was the Sunday School superintendent at her little church. People in the community loved her. A truly wonderful woman, she held that church together many times through her prayers and confidence in Jesus. She was a little giant, really! A ball of fire for Jesus.

We know that sickness is no respecter of people, nor is it a respecter of age. Mildred's health failed, and she had to be taken to the hospital. After many tests, they found that she had a heart condition. Mildred, although up in years, was just a little child in Jesus. She believed in God and trusted him. She had put her life in God's hands. Her prayer was, "Father, whatever comes my way, I know you, the Lord of my life, will take care of it." She went from one hospital to another, from one doctor to another, where they treated her as best they could. They knew she wasn't going to live a long time. They knew her days were numbered, so they'd patch her up and send her home.

"Very Sick"

Then one day they took her to the hospital, and they kept her there. She was very sick. Later that evening she had an unexpected visitor. Jesus came right into her room, sat beside her bed and said, "Mildred, I'm coming for you soon." She said, "You are, Jesus? If that's the case, Jesus, I'll just wait right here for you." She then told all the nurses, "Jesus is coming for me. He came and told me so. He told me that he's going to take me home real soon."

Mildred's pastor came to visit her, and she said to him, "Brother, do I owe you anything?" He said, "No, Sister, you don't owe me anything." She kept telling everyone who crossed her path, "Jesus is coming for me." Finally she called one of the nurses in and said, "Would you make sure that my face is washed and my hair is combed, because I'm going to go home today, praise God. Jesus is coming for me this very day!"

O death, where is thy sting? O grave, where is thy victory? (1 Corinthians 15:55). Mildred went to the Lord on Sunday. On the Lord's Day, he came, and he took her home. Hallelujah! That's how close we can be to Jesus.

"I'm Going Home"

I think of a song that we wrote a little while ago about an old man seated in his rocking chair in a house that he'd owned since he was a young man. He'd given his son the house because his age didn't allow him to keep it up anymore. He said to his son, "I'm going home today, son." He rocked his chair gently back and forth. His son said, "Dad, this is your home. It always has been and it always will be as long as you live."

"No, son," he said. "I'm talking about Jesus and my home beyond the clouds. And son, do you see him? There he is, he's coming for me now." All of a sudden that rocking chair stopped, and that old thin body just sat there. All that remained was just a shell. His spirit had gone on to be with his savior. That's how close we can be to Jesus. Just like sister Mildred. Amen.

She ran life's race and finished a winner. Her prize is a place at the feet of Jesus.

In the beginning of this book we dedicated it to three special sisters in the Lord. Each of them we considered . . .

A Saint

His word reads, "Go ye therefore . . . " (Matthew 28:19). Go tell the good news, amen; yes, go share what he has done for you. That is what we did. We're living proof that our God truly supplies ". . . all our need . . . " (Phillipians 4:19). We have seen many strange, wonderful blessings directly from the mighty hand of God, and we've made many lasting friendships.

Several years ago, we began to send out newsletters, short stories, really, about how God was moving at our revivals. One dear saint we wrote to was sister Ethel Gorman, a transplanted Bostonian who wound up living in Canada's ocean playground, Nova Scotia. We went to visit her one time when we were ministering in her area, and she said, "Jerry, are you saving a copy of those letters you're sending me?"

"No, Ethel. I wish I had, but no I haven't," I replied.

"Well," she said, "I've saved every one for you for when you write the book."

I responded with, "Sister Ethel, I'm not going to write any book."

But she, in her positive, matter-of-fact way said, "Yes, you are." Then she went on, "When I die, they'll all be here. Make sure you get them." Then she paused, as if thinking, and said, "No, better yet, you take them with you today."

So she gave me those letters and from then on I saved a copy every month. Time sure flies. Years have gone by as we continued on for Jesus. We were up in the Northwest Territories ministering at a native camp meeting. God was moving mightily with healings of all sorts. One man who had been in a major car accident came. He had suffered much. It was a miracle that he had even survived. Many of his bones had been broken. He was still in serious pain after several months and unable to work. Using a cane, he painfully made his way to the service. We prayed, "Lord, heal him from head to toe, for you are a restoring Savior. Please touch him. All glory to you, Lord." When the power of God hit him, he fell to the floor and lay there as God's healing power began to put him back together again. Bones snapped back in place as he was *totally healed*. He left the meeting astonished at what God had done for him, a miracle, indeed. He now has a testimony that could lead many to Jesus.

About that time, it came into my spirit, "You've got to write the book." I tried, but I could not escape the Holy Spirit who kept nudging my inner man telling me, "You've got to write the book."

For some reason, I phoned back to where Ethel lived and received the news that at about the time it was impressed upon my heart to write the book, Sister Ethel had gone on to be with Jesus. So without a doubt, I knew I had to do it. I consider it a great blessing to add this little chapter in memory of a saint in Jesus, Sister Saint Ethel, amen.

There is nothing the Holy Spirit cannot do, as you will read in . . .

Good Morning, Holy Spirit

===≈≈≈≈≈≈===

They're back again, Annie," I whispered. "Look, they're watching us . . . .don't move a muscle or they'll disappear!" We watched, marveling at the sleek beauty of several wild mule deer grazing on the parsonage lawn.

"How many are there, Jerry?" Annie whispered.

"Six—no, maybe seven. I think there's a buck out beside the hedge."

On Saturday, we arrived in John Day, Oregon, a small mountain town surrounded by high desert, now parched by constant sunshine and relentless dry winds. We noticed a sign that indicated the fire hazard was extreme—"Be careful—a match could burn our home," it read with a life-size picture of Smoky the Bear.

Consequently, the mule deer, driven by thirst and hunger, came closer to us than they wanted to be. Ah, yes, seven. That is a buck, a big old boy, out by the hedge. Then I sneezed, and as suddenly as they appeared, they vanished.

We had held services in John Day, but were detained waiting for our mail. The pastor, who drove a wood chip truck to supplement his wages from the church, said to me, "Jerry, go ahead—use my office—it's yours! Feel right at home." So I did.

It was quiet inside the church, and a good place to pray. As I sat in the office, it came to me, "Hey, I haven't written a song for a long, long time! Amen," I thought. "That's true, I'm about as dry as that old desert." I pushed the thought out of my mind and began meditating on the Holy Spirit. Jesus himself said he'd send another Comforter. He can do all things! Then the thought hit me, "Why not ask him (the Holy Spirit) to write a song?" (See Luke 11:9.) So I did. I invited him to come and co-write a song to lift up our mutual best friend, Jesus. And the words began to flow like a stream.

> Good morning, Holy Spirit!
> Time for us to start another day,
> Good morning, Holy Spirit,
> Come and be my guide along life's way.

A bubbling stream of words, along with a melody as fresh as the morning dew. I picked up a guitar and began playing the song directly off the hot coals of heaven. Almost instantly, the chorus came.

> Walk with me, talk with me, Holy Spirit,
> Dine with me, shine through me,
> All day long, keep me strong,
> Good morning, Holy Spirit.
> I thank the Father for sending you
> To glorify the Son.

As I finished writing the last stanza, Annie's voice echoed through the church, "Lunch is ready! Jerry, it's lunch time!"

"Never mind lunch Annie," I said. "Listen to this new song God gave me."

She sat and listened as I sang it to her. Later, she confided that the air was charged with the Spirit (perhaps as Brother Moses had sensed when he was instructed to take off his shoes—". . . holy ground" (Exodus 3:5).

Since then we've recorded the song in Nashville. Sister Annie suggested we use birds chirping to start the song. We did, and it became even more unique. People have written from different parts of the world to obtain a copy.

We believe the Holy Spirit worked with John Newton when "Amazing Grace" was written, and for sure God was there in John Day, Oregon, when "Good Morning, Holy Spirit" was born.

FOOTNOTE

There's a book by Pastor Benny Hinn entitled, *Good Morning, Holy Spirit*. We read and enjoyed it as have countless millions of others. We believe you'll be blessed with this song, also. Included is an order form and instructions near the end of this book. *Jerry and Annie*.

Once upon a time, we prayed: "Lord, send laborers for the harvest," and he sent us! (See John 4:35.)

The Holy Spirit is still recruiting laborers. Don't be surprised when he calls you.

He sees the hearts on both sides of the tracks and becons them to come. He is a life changing Savior. Sometimes he reaches way down to the very bottom of . . .

The Pits—Our Testimony

〰〰〰

"Permanently institutionalized or suicide," the authoritative voice of the psychiatrist said. "That's my prognosis. But who knows for sure? They're coming up with new drugs all the time, and, of course, sometime shock treatment works."

Through the fogginess enveloping my brain, the revelation came that this was me they were talking about. Me. Yes, me. What a life! Such a mixed up mess. I'm hooked on prescription drugs. I drink, gamble, and smoke. And my husband's as bad as me, even worse. He's a hopeless alcoholic. We've got two children living in this horrible mess, and now these doctors are saying I'm crazy. It must be true. After all, I'm confined to this hospital.

"Phone call, Mrs. Shaw," the nurse informed me. "It's your sister from Toronto."

"Annie, it's Joan, your sister! I just called home and they told me that you were in the hospital, so I had to call." She talked a blue streak. "Annie, all you really need is Jesus. He can heal you, he can set you free!"

"Now hold on, Joan. Stop right there. If you ever want to speak to me again don't talk to me about that foolishness."

One of God's many gifts is wisdom. Joan used her gift, said, "OK," and switched the subject to other things. Much, much later, I found out that she went to church and asked her born-again prayer group to lift me up to Jesus in prayer; to storm heaven for me.

THE QUESTION

How our marriage even survived to this point is nearly impossible to understand. Jerry was not only a chronic alcoholic, but booze turned him into a mean and abusive man. He and his cronies met many nights to drown themselves in whisky and rum. What a hateful situation we were in! There were no happy campers in our home.

A PLAN

"The next time I get out of the hospital, I'm going to leave Jerry," I thought.

One day I saw a man in much worse condition than me with a suitcase in his hand, signing a book at the reception desk. I checked it out and found that I, too, could sign myself out. Seems that no one could be held against their will. A light went on inside me. "I'm going to sign myself out of this hospital, and I'm going to sign myself right out of my hopeless marriage," I thought.

So I did. Then I phoned Jerry, telling him to come and pick me up.

"I'm coming home," I said.

FEET TO MY PLAN

Once at home, I put my plan in motion. I said, "Jerry, it's over." My head pounded. What a mess I was in. My mouth was dry. "We've got to split up. We're destroying each other. It has to end."

Jerry agreed. "We should separate," he said, adding that he loved me.

"Ridiculous," I thought. "There's no love lost in this relationship." He drove me to the train station, and I breathed easier as it pulled out. Alcohol allowed the miles to slip quickly behind me, and later that night, the train connected with a boat bound for Newfoundland. We were many miles out to sea in the Gulf when the spirit of suicide flooded me. I had just enough alcohol in me to consider it. I thought, "I'll make my way up to the top deck and find myself a spot to jump off. They'll never miss me . . . I'll be out of this mess of a life."

But God had another plan. A woman began to walk with me, matching me step for step. And talk. Oh, that woman could talk to the point that I could no longer think straight. You never know who God will use, after all. He has the whole world in his hands, sinners and saints alike. It was a long trip, but finally I arrived at my parent's home in Grand Bank. What a state of confusion I was in. So many unanswered questions. This was not my life's plan, breaking up my marriage, even divorce. And what about my children? What should I do next?

I'd only been gone about a week when Jerry began calling. "Decisions must be made," he said. "Our children, the house . . . the legalities of separation and divorce. Everything's up in the air," he said. "We just can't leave it there."

After his last call, I sorted through my thoughts, and suddenly, I felt a strong urge to phone him. So I dialed his number and found myself saying, "If you believe there's any hope for this marriage, then come here and we'll talk." He in turn said, "Annie, I'm running the restaurant, looking after the kids. It would be much easier if you came here."

HEADED HOME

This time, as I traveled back to Jerry and the children, I wondered what lay ahead. In the past, we'd been like two trains on the same track, one going east and the other going west. Yet, here I am returning. Maybe I am crazy. What am I doing?

"Next stop, Campbellton," the conductor yelled, as the train slowed and the platform came into sight. And there stood my husband, Jerry, waiting for me. We held each other and hugged, then loaded my luggage and drove toward home. I turned to Jerry, and said, "We need to find a church to go to," and he readily agreed.

Some folks invited us to come to their church, so we did. It wasn't long before I was asked to join the choir, and I received all the benefits, one of which was a lobster party one Sunday afternoon. While there, a church member asked my husband if he wanted a cold beer. This really surprised Jerry. Somehow he felt that alcohol and religion did not mix.

Shortly after that, the church closed for the summer. God knows our hearts. He wants us to seek him. One day in the restaurant, a young lady named Martha said, "Jerry, you'd like it at our church. They even play guitar there." She knew that Jerry played music and had a band. God knows just how to pull the right strings. He sure had Jerry's attention!

"Imagine that!" Jerry said. "A church where they play guitars! I'm going to check it out."

So together, Jerry and our son, ventured into a full gospel church, into a Holy Ghost meeting. Born-again people speaking in other tongues; the whole nine yards! Right into a powerful service that would make any sinner edgy, and both Jerry and my son were unsaved. It finally ended with the altar call as the pastor dismissed those who had to leave. Jerry was quick to take our son and head for the door.

"Son," he said, "That's our first and last trip to that church. What did you think of it?"

"Oh, I kind of liked it, Dad," he said.

Back at the house, Annie pumped us for tidbits of Pentecost. "Did they swing on the chandeliers? Did they roll in the aisle? I've heard stories," she said. "They're weird, I've heard."

"Yes, yes, they're different, Annie. You wouldn't like it there. Your nerves are too bad. Their elevators don't go to the top floor. Myself, I don't plan to go there again, either."

But when Sunday came, I was shocked to find out that's where Annie wanted to go. So I gulped and we headed for church. The church was close to full, and we were forced to sit up close to the front, just three rows back. The preacher, Milford Heinbecker, seemed to know all about us. In fact, his whole sermon was about us. No question whatsoever, we were rank sinners. He hit the nail on the head—ouch! We began to bicker and squabble right there in church. About that time, the pastor gave the altar call, and Annie jumped to her feet, hurrying towards the door. But the pull of the Holy Spirit drew her toward the altar. She ran and knelt down in the presence of God Almighty. A woman of the church came quickly, put her arms around her and led her to Jesus. What a transformation! Annie was saved! A true, 100% born-again experience. And me? I was still unsaved.

It's hard to live in a house with a new Christian. Annie used to be flat out for the devil. Now she was sold out, on fire for Jesus. She wanted everything God had to offer. Everything.

RETROSPECT

Before Jesus came into her life, Annie was an avid bingo player. Sometimes several nights a week, she'd be found sitting with others like herself, hooked on the game. I used to lay in bed next to her and after she fell asleep I'd begin calling out numbers, like B-1, I-16, N-31, G-57, O-75. After a while, she'd sit right up in bed and yell, "Bingo!" but she never woke up.

All that ended with her salvation, as did her dependence on alcohol and tobacco. She indeed was born again. Yes, she was saved to the uttermost. One night after she fell asleep, she rose on one elbow and began to speak in other tongues. And at our restaurant, she filled the ashtrays with tiny red Bibles. At the cash register, she passed out Bible tracks. Amen, Annie had changed!

The church was in the midst of a Holy Ghost revival. Thirty-nine new Christians were seated in the front rows, all hungry for more of God. Annie told the pastor what had happened in her sleep. He said, "Sounds like the Holy Spirit baptized you. Perhaps he'll do it again." So he prayed, he and the others as well. Suddenly, a wind blew across the front of the church. Annie's head shot up and she began speaking in other tongues. One by one every one of the new born-again Christians were filled with the Holy Spirit. Truly heaven came down and glory filled their souls.

Jerry's Testimony

I was still unsaved. Oh, I was going through the motions all right, but the only one I was fooling was me. I couldn't enter in. I was just a pew-warmer.

But God Had a Plan

Our friend, Don West, and his wife had just moved up from Maine. They invited us to their home for an evening meal. After supper was finished, we polished off a bottle of whiskey together. Then out of the blue, Don said, "Hey, there's a healing service in Campbellton tonight. Do you want to go? It starts at seven."

"Sure," I said. "I've always wanted to see what that can of worms is about."

Around that time, the pastor showed up along with his wife, and we crowded into a car for the twenty-mile trip to the healing revival. We entered the church and found the only seats available were in the back row.

They sang, they exhorted, they clapped their hands, they raised their arms, some people spoke in tongues, others prophesied. What a service! The evangelist, Reverend Lenny Anderson from North Carolina, moved in the gifts of the Spirit. Time was forgotten as all heaven broke loose. The healing service started close to ten o'clock.

Retrospectively

I need to back track just a little. Many people had come in need of healing, and I was one of them. I had hurt my back while working at Ford Motor Company. I had a slipped disc that never got better. Truth is, it got worse. Sometimes I was in excruciating pain, to the point where I'd turn gray as I attempted to rise to my feet. Sometimes, I'd have to slide off the chair, onto my knees, and then somehow I'd manage to get to my feet from that position. What a mess!

But God knows all. The Holy Spirit was using an evangelist to tell everyone there was a man in the last row with a bad back. He was pointing a long bony finger at me. I thought, "He can't mean me, can he? How would he know?" I even looked behind me, but sure enough, I was in the last row. Indeed, I was the man in question.

The evangelist spoke. "If you will rise up and come to Jesus, God will heal you." I thought, "Well, what do I have to lose? Maybe God would heal me." About then, a loud voice inside said, "Smarten up, don't be so foolish. This is nothing but a farce, a joke. You're an idiot if you believe any of this. Don't be so gullible. This is insanity." But another voice said, "Rise up and come to me. I am the God that healeth thee." I found myself walking forward to the altar and to Jesus.

They sat me down in a straight-backed chair and the evangelist, sure of his God, called the ministers and priests to come to witness a miracle about to happen. Then he held both of my feet in his hands, pointing out that my left leg was shorter than the other.

"This is the cause of your back problem," he said. He began to pray for me, and I in turn closed my eyes, as if to help him. Suddenly he stopped praying, and said, "The Lord has told me to tell you to open your eyes. He wants you to see what he's going to do for you." So I looked on as he again prayed. Finally he said, "Now, Lord, cause his leg to grow!" My leg began to tingle and very slowly grew longer.

A shiver ran through me. I knew I was in the presence of God. I started to get hot and cold at the same time. God surly had my full attention. The evangelist prayed for the healing of my back, and then he took me by the hand and pulled me to my feet.

"Walk to the door and back," he said. "Check out what the Lord has done."

So I did. I walked without pain and stood straight as an arrow. Yes, God had healed me! Yes, I bent my knee to the King of Kings that night. Yes, alcohol was a thing of my past. Yes, I was set free! I said yes, yes, yes! to Jesus.

One by one, the scales of the past began to be scraped away. Alcohol—over, finished, through. Cussing—gone. Tobacco—yesterday's habit. The crutches of sin broken by Christ's conquering love, and each area that he cleaned, he filled with his love and compassion.

A New Family

Of course our old friends labeled us temporarily insane. Religious fanatics. Most of them wrote us off. We were told many of them predicted, "It won't last long. It's just a phase they're going through." But it did last, praise the Lord. God reached down and lifted us up nineteen years ago, and, amen, we're still saved; on fire for Jesus. He cleaned us up and put us on the road to go tell the good things he's done for us. We've ministered in countless churches, on street corners, Indian reservations, prisons, senior's homes, as well as on radio and television outreaches, and now there is this book that we pray will reach and help many to cry out to Jesus for a life-changing experience.

FOOTNOTE

Friend, as Annie's sister said, "All you need is Jesus."
No matter how far down you are, no matter how hopeless your life seems to be. Even if you think you could
never be free from drugs or alcohol, take heart friend.
God is no respecter of persons. He did it for us, and he
can do it for you. He knows all about you. He knows
how deep in sin you are, and he's waiting to hear your
heart cry for help. His nail-scarred hand will reach down
and help you to escape your pit, amen.

To have your own personalized prayed over copy of

The Miracle Road

simply write me at the address below:
Annie Shaw
3362 Nina Rd.
White Pine, TN 37890

or in Canada write me at
Annie Shaw
56 Keith Lane RR1
Lawrencetown (Valley)
Nova Scotia, BOS1MO
Canada

or to order by phone have your
credit card ready and call

(800) 917-BOOK

$10.95 (US) or $16.95 (Canada)
plus $3.95 shipping and handling

Dear Annie,
   I would like to order a copy of your album
   Good Morning Holy Spirit

   Please mail it to
   Mr/Mrs _____
   Street address _____
   State/Provence _____
   Postal code _____

   ❑ Cassette
        or
   ❑ CD

Enclosed is my love gift of $_____ Plus postage.

Our other cassette albums are:

"The Old Man and God"
"Pray 'em on Home"
"Thanks Lord"
"Here Comes Jesus"
"Good Morning Holy Spirit"

(I WANT TO BE AN EVANGELIST) 1 Timothy 4:5

I just finished reading *The Miracle Road* and truely believe a copy of this Book **must** be placed in the hands of the spiritually underprivileged. Every federal prison, county jail, Indian tribe, Eskimo band, unwed mothers home, AIDS center, detox unit, and seniors home in the United States, Canada, and beyond needs this life changing book! Yes, I realize it will cost! But I feel led to enclose a one time gift of $_____

I'd like to make a monthly pledge of $_____

Please pin your needs to the cross.
Phillippians 4:19
Mail it to us
and we'll believe with you for your
VICTORY!

Please write:
Annie Shaw
3362 Nina Road
White Pine, TN 37890

In Canada:
Annie Shaw
56 Keith Lane RR1
Lawrencetown (Valley)
Nova Scotia, B0S1M0
Canada

Please, add my name to your daily prayer list.
Name: _____
Address: _____
City or Town: _____
Country: _____
Zip Code: _____